The Coaching Philosophies of
Louis van Gaal
and the
Ajax Coaches

by
Henny Kormelink
Tjeu Seeverens

Library of Congress Cataloging - in - Publication Data

Kormelink, Henny; Seeverens, Tjeu
The Coaching Philosophies of Louis van Gaal and the Ajax Coaches/Henny Kormelink,
    Tjeu Seeverens

ISBN No. 1-890946-03-6
Library of Congress Catalog Number - 97-068500
Copyright © 1997 "De VoetbalTrainer"

This book was originally published by "De VoetbalTrainer", a publication of Uitgeverij
Eisma bv, P.O. Box 340, 8901 BC Leeuwarden, The Netherlands

Reedswain books are available at special discounts for bulk purchase. For details, contact
the Special Sales Manager at Reedswain at 1-800-331-5191.

Printed in the United States of America.

Credits: Art Direction, Cover Design and Layout • Kimberly N. Bender
Photographs/Diagrams: "De VoetbalTrainer"
Cover Photos: Louis van de Vuurst

Introduction

Amsterdam is known throughout the world as a center of creativity. A place where the boundaries of freedom are constantly redrawn. Where the limits of political, cultural and social behavior are dynamically explored. A city that repeatedly pushes ahead, consolidates new ground, then surges forward again.

This is a fertile climate for the development of soccer skills. It is why Amsterdam is Ajax, and Ajax is Amsterdam. This is the club that gave the young Johan Cruyff, one of the greatest soccer players of all time, the scope to develop his fantastic talent. At many other clubs his physical frailties and know it all attitude would have been reason enough to cast him aside with the legion of other young hopefuls who are never heard of again. At Ajax, however, daring, nerve, willfulness, creativity, ingenuity and technique are rated higher than slavish adherence to rigid systems of tactics or simple physical strength.

This did not just apply to Cruyff. Anyone who is privileged enough to spend time at the club's training complex soon learns that flair on the ball and an abundance of technique are the selection criteria. From the 6 and 7 year-olds to the seniors.

The typical Ajax combination of technique, insight, personality and speed of

action is best expressed in creative and, therefore, attacking soccer. This is Ajax's inviolable philosophy. Everywhere in the world a winning coach is fêted and celebrated. In Amsterdam, however, mere success in not enough. Ever since the English coach, Jack Reynolds, made Ajax a fortress of attacking soccer in the years before the Second World War (1934-1940), all other concepts have been rejected. Tomislav Ivic was a coach who gained success and honors throughout the world, and in 1977, in his first season at Ajax, the club won the national championship. Unfortunately this success was based on defensive tactics, and this was the reason for Ivic's premature dismissal.

To play attacking soccer, to dare to take risks, to accept nothing but the best in terms of expressing this philosophy on the field, and to win prizes every year. This has been the almost impossible combination of demands faced by every Ajax coach down the years. It is therefore no surprise to find that most coaches have left, or been forced to leave, after only one or two years.

In fact only four coaches have been successful in recent decades, and these were Rinus Michels, Stefan Kovacs, Johan Cruyff and Louis van Gaal.

Michels conquered the whole soccer world between 1965 and 1971 by introducing "total soccer." Michel's Ajax consistently played sublime soccer and was rewarded with four national championships, as well as winning the national cup three times, and the European Cup once. This achievement and his major contribution to the success of the Dutch national team brought Michels a degree of respect and admiration throughout the world that endures to this day.

The taciturn Michels was succeeded by the talkative and knowledgeable Romanian, Stefan Kovacs (1971-1973). In this period Ajax won the national championship, the national cup competition, and the European Cup (all twice), and the European Supercup. These triumphs were followed by a lean period, before Johan Cruyff took charge from 1985 to 1988 and won a prize each year, carrying off the Dutch cup in two of them and the European Cup Winners' Cup in the other.

The final, and by far the most successful, member of this quartet is their last coach, Louis van Gaal. As a professional soccer player he was known for his confidence in his own opinions, his ability to convince players and coaches alike that he was right, and above all for his tactical insight. In 1988 these characteristics gained him the position of youth coordinator at Ajax. When coach Kurt Lindner departed after only a few months, Van Gaal and the current youth coach, Spitz Kohn, temporarily took charge of the first team. Ajax's board of directors felt that it was too soon to offer Van Gaal the job permanently and engaged the articulate Leo Beenhakker. Don Leo won the national championship with Ajax, but then brought down the wrath of the Ajax board on his head when he cashed in on this success by signing a lucrative contract with Real Madrid in mid-season.

And so, in 1991, his assistant Van Gaal was given a second chance as an interim solution, until Cruyff returned, as many people thought at the time. The reality proved to be completely different. Nothing daunted, the new young coach immediately began to prune his first team squad. Established stars such as Jonk, Wouters, Roy and Bergkamp were either allowed to leave or told that there was no longer a place for them. They were all firm favorites with the fans and it was not long before the critics began to sharpen their knives. This was the start of a permanent love-hate relationship between Van Gaal and the Dutch press. Step by step, however, Van Gaal proved that he was right. He faced up squarely to the demanding task, and in just a few years he advanced from youth coordinator to the best coach in the Netherlands.

The Ajax of Louis van Gaal. The story of a coach who, with scintillating soccer, made his club world champion, winner of European Cup I, winner of the UEFA Cup, winner of the European Supercup, threefold national champion, winner of the Dutch cup competition, and triple winner of the Dutch Supercup. This book analyzes the unbelievable success of a perfectionist at a unique club.

Forward

Eleven major trophies with an international ambience in scarcely six years. This is the unique achievement of Louis van Gaal. A coach who has so much success with a top club such as Ajax at the very start of his career must be a extraordinary coach with a very special approach.

Famous coaches rarely feel the urge to reveal their coaching secrets to the outside world. In a sense, Van Gaal is no exception, for his relationship with the media has frequently been strained.

However, the new coach of Barcelona was always prepared to make an exception for the authors of this unique book, the knowledgeable Dutch soccer writers Henny Kormelink and Tjeu Seeverens. Once each year he granted them an interview, during which he would explain how Ajax functioned, right down to the smallest details. He also gave them permission to talk to other coaches on the Ajax staff. The writers have now translated the many hours of analysis, explanation and inside information into a remarkable book that will enthrall everyone with knowledge of soccer, from start to finish.

There has never been a book like this, in which a famous soccer coach with an international reputation reveals so many of his secrets. There is no room for peripherals. This is a book about the genuine essentials of the game of soccer. It is a remarkable document, of interest to the whole soccer world.

Egbert van Hes
Publisher of De Voetbal Trainer

Contents

Chapter 1
The Basis of
Van Gaal's Philosophy

In a city where freedom is a historic right, Van Gaal preached discipline from his very first day at Ajax. Indeed, it became the basis of the Van Gaal philosophy.

"Soccer is a team sport, and the members of the team are therefore dependent on each other. If certain players do not carry out their tasks properly on the pitch, then their colleagues will suffer. This means that each player has to carry out his basic tasks to the best of his ability, and this requires a disciplined approach on the pitch. In my opinion this can only be achieved if there is also discipline off the pitch. When you stand in front of a group of players as a coach, you first have to create the right framework, by explaining what discipline involves, and what you understand by it. It is largely a question of details: being in the dressing room thirty minutes before a training session starts; keeping your things neat and tidy; sitting at the table to eat together, and not reading a newspaper while doing so; looking after your body; and being on the team bus punctually after a game. If a player does not accept this, then first of all I have a talk with him. I try to reason with him, and I only impose a fine as a last resort, because it is an admission of weakness on the part of a coach.

The process of imbuing discipline as a matter of course within the squad progressed very quickly after my appointment. I think this was because most of the players were already familiar with me as a coach, from the period when Kohn and I were in charge of the team. They knew what to expect. This was certainly a big advantage. From the very start, my objective was for the squad itself to react to any threat to team discipline. I achieved this objective in my first season. The assistant coaches thought they could sometimes arrive a few minutes late, but the squad soon called them to order. And from the beginning the players themselves ensured that they were all back in the bus on time. I no longer have to tell them to stay on after a training session is finished; that has become a matter of course. I could come up with lots of similar examples. I think it is an advantage that I myself possess a lot of self-discipline. It is a part of my character, and that is crucial if you preach self-discipline to others."

Communication

"The second element of my philosophy is communication. Here, too, I first had to create the necessary framework. At the outset I engineered situations in which players were obligated, step by step, to communicate with each other and with the coaching staff. Monday is an important day in this context. The medical treatment sessions on this day were extended when I took over, because this is one of the occasions when players talk to each other spontaneously. There is also a detailed postmortem of the last match. In the early days the discussion was, as at many clubs, more of a monologue by the coach, i.e. myself. Thanks to my approach, the first reactions quickly followed, and genuine dialogues were soon taking place. Progress was very fast in this field, too.

In a normal week there are, of course, more of these moments. Each training session is a form of communication. The drills themselves are not so important, it is more a question of what you do with them. During training sessions the players see what a coach wants. I often stop the practice games and challenge the players to think about the soccer problems they are facing. Thanks to my eleven years as a teacher, I have enough experience to know whether I need to step in or keep quiet, and who to talk to. Naturally I explain more to youngsters than to an experienced player of 30, who is set in many of his ways and is probably incapable of changing them.

The media frequently portray me as an authoritarian figure, who thinks he knows it all. The people who work with me daily know better. I learn something new every day from the people around me. From the players, the medical staff, my assistants Gerard van der Lem, Bobby Haarms and goalkeeper coach Frans Hoek. On Thursdays we discuss each individual player with the whole support team. I also ask everyone to say what he feels about the previous game and what he thinks about the next opponent. I talk to players every day. It is then my task as the leader of that team - and I very definitely count the players as part of it - to make a selection from all the information available and to decide on the course to be taken. I then expect everyone to support this course in public, because to do otherwise is simply asking for problems."

Team-building

"Discipline and continuous communication with each other inevitably lead to team-building. When I introduced the term to the Dutch soccer world in my first season, a number of Dutch journalists promptly made fun of me. One newspaper, for example, published a photo in which the players and I were holding hands in a ring while playing a game of headers. The caption was accompanied by a mocking remark about the term 'team-building.' But carrying out such an exercise while holding hands is no more than a small cog in a large wheel. In soccer, everything depends on the team aspect. It is therefore important that each player knows what the others can and can't do. You have to discover each other's skills, and this automatically leads to a good mutual understanding, which is the basis for the result. All players have to learn to put the team's interests first. Team-building is not ensuring that you all like each other, but that you learn about each other's skills and can talk to each other about them. It is an offshoot of communication and discipline.

Do you know when it became clear to me that the Ajax players realized this?

On the evening before the important European Cup game against AA Gent (Belgium), also in my first season. At that time John Van Loen was one of the Ajax strikers. I asked him what he thought was the best system to play against the solid Belgian team. John replied "4:3:3, coach." He knew very well that he would not be picked if we played this system, but at such an important moment, John put the interests of the team first. That gives a coach enormous satisfaction.

I repeat, it is all about discipline and communication. And naturally the overall concept has to be right. Those are the three foundation stones of my work at Ajax. The concept is that we have to sell a product, and that product is attacking and attractive soccer. The best system for doing this is 3:4:3, because the players and the coaching staff fully support it. We agree things together and then we go out and do them together. That is how we work at Ajax, and this is clearly recognizable.

This recognizability is also one of the 'secrets' of Ajax's success. You could call it the club's 'house style.' I once heard the AC Madrid coach Capello give a lecture for all Dutch professional soccer team coaches, in which he spoke about the typical club culture of AC Milan. I saw certain parallels between my vision and that of Capello. He spoke of the 'we' feeling at AC Milan, and of how the players who had come through the club's own youth policy, such as Costacurta and Maldini, regard themselves as guardians of the club's individual culture. Players who come from outside have to adjust themselves to this culture, and if they don't, they cannot succeed, no matter how good they are. Capello mentioned Savicevic as an example; even this top player needed two years to adjust to the typical Milan culture.

This is also how it is at Ajax. Players who have received their soccer education at Ajax and are now established in the first team, act as guardians of the typical Ajax style, and I encourage that. Players who come from outside have to make the adjustment. This is why newcomers usually find life difficult at first. Players who are stars elsewhere would fail at Ajax if they could not adjust to the club's style, both on and off the field of play. This explains how a talented youngster from the club's own ranks can be preferred to a player such as Santos, who had been in Brazil's World Cup winning side. Outsiders often find this incomprehensible. But inside the club everyone is familiar with the Ajax 'feeling,' because almost everyone who works behind the scenes once played for Ajax, and therefore grew up with the Ajax culture. Everyone knows what is on offer here. No matter where you go within the club, you will meet people whose hearts beat faster for Ajax. That is the club's great strength."

Chapter 2
Van Gaal, The Innovator

Under Louis van Gaal, Ajax soon became a pioneer of innovative ideas in soccer.

"It is true that I have been given the scope to try things in a way that would be impossible at other clubs. I have my own ideas about fitness training. The good physical condition of the side as we approach the end of the season is no coincidence. But I first had to stick my neck out. It is important how you train: do you want players to be mentally fit or do you just aim to ensure that they are in good physical condition?

Another crucial element, in my opinion, is that we at Ajax follow a completely different physiological approach. The exercise physiologist Jos Geysel, an external specialist, convinced me on this matter. His vision of physical training is totally different to that which we were taught in coaching courses.

We used to be taught that endurance was ever so important as a basis for soccer players. Geysel maintains that you acquire a different type of muscle tissue if you concentrate too much on endurance work. It is therefore important to avoid excess acidification at the start of the preparation period, and to allow players to do interval training (in doses) at an early stage. I started with this three years ago.

The players find it very enjoyable. It's less strenuous and boring than all that endless running. I should know. I remember my own days as a player. I was always at the back when we did endurance training. On a good day I could just about keep up. On the field, however, I used to run more than the other players. At least, that's the way I saw it. It's a question of having the right attitude towards matches and a good soccer brain; knowing where the ball is going to go. Ajax trains its players to run as little as possible on the field. That way you're much quicker at picking out the more important features of the game.

Jos Geysel had already used this approach successfully with field hockey players, and he was able to convince me. Nevertheless, as the coach of a top team you need a lot of courage to take such a step, especially as it flies in the face of existing theories.

Then you have to convert the rest of the coaching staff. You talk it through with the entire backroom staff and try to convince them. At the end of the day, of course, it's my decision, but it's much better if you know you have the support of the rest of the staff. I attach a lot of value to working together as a team. I see it as my job to come up with new initiatives. I then have to control that process and provide leadership."

Notebook

Louis van Gaal was one of the first Dutch coaches to take a soccer notebook with him into the dug-out during the game.

"We only introduce new initiatives at Ajax if we can put them into practice. I could illustrate the story by telling you about team-building or by using the handy modern projector which I always have with me at discussions.

The soccer notebook I always have with me in the dug-out attracts a lot of remarks. For me it's an extremely valuable aid, so it's not important what other people think. First I always jot down the collective mistakes that go against the pre-planned tactics. For example, the fact that Litmanen would be more effective if he played 5 yards further upfield, because this would have immediate consequences for Blind and Rijkaard, who would also have to push up a few yards. That's the most important aspect. Next, I always note down individual mistakes of course. This way I have a logical sequence of aspects about which I can talk to the players during the interval. That's why I find a list so useful. The chance of forgetting something important is negligible.

In addition I use my notes for the post-match team talk, for other forms of communication with players, and of course for putting together the drills for the training sessions after the game is over. If you don't put pen to paper, it is more likely that you'll forget something."

Post-match team talk

"I believe that a team-talk after the game is also important. You can indicate exactly what went well and what went badly. You can pick out particular individuals, but you can also address the group as a whole. Above all, the group process is important to me. If, in the team talk, I pick out the strengths of a given individual, the other players must be able to accept this. An extensive post-match team talk teaches a player about team discipline and self-discipline, individual responsibility and collective responsibility. Only then does the whole become more than the sum of the parts!

In an important game against Bayern Munich, Ajax player Frank de Boer told off the young Patrick Kluivert in no uncertain terms in front of millions of viewers, and Kluivert reacted strongly. That is a typical subject of discussion during the post-match team talk. In effect, Frank de Boer was right. By not sticking to the agreed game plan, Kluivert risked the team's prospects. As a coach, it's satisfying to see your players responding directly on the field. Kluivert reacted very emotionally, which is fine by me. After all, soccer is all about emotion. The next day, however, I expect Kluivert to be able to respond in a rational way again. He'll then admit that he was wrong. At that moment it is a question of forgive and forget. Although you know that the media will blow it out of proportion afterwards, as a top club you have to learn to live with this."

Video

"The video is only rarely switched on during the discussion. I make less use of videos, especially for domestic league games. For these games I'm usually more occupied with preparing my own team. I have every detail on Dutch opponents in my head, and so do most of the Ajax players.

When we play European clubs it's somewhat different and I regularly use videos for preparations. The players' information is more limited as well, so it's useful to use tapes to demonstrate important details like, for example, fixed patterns of play. I don't just pick out specific details from a game. For example, watching a tape of a whole first half is usually more worthwhile than just picking out a few highlights. In that way you can figure out why a team adopted certain tactics, and then you can examine them.

I don't place much value on the popular videos showing the best goals scored by strikers. I always look at strikers in relation to the team as a whole. When is a striker most alert, how does he react in certain situations, and what are his fixed patterns of play? I try continually to get Ajax players to watch games in this way. If you make them aware of this as often as possible, they automatically start to look at games on television differently."

Tactics

As far as tactics are concerned, Van Gaal also has his own ideas.

"Many sides play man-to-man marking at the back, with each defender following his direct opponent as closely as possible. Ajax nearly always plays a positional zonal marking game, with defenders staying in position and picking up an opponent when he comes into their zone. That only applies during the passive phase, of course. In the active phase they obviously follow their man when the ball is in their vicinity. I always refer to the Ajax defenders who have to take out the opposition's strikers as the 'killers'. That is an indication of what I expect of them.

In modern soccer the players in the middle of the back four - the numbers 3 and 4 - have really become the playmakers. That's why Blind is, and Rijkaard was, so important to Ajax. The number 10, behind the strikers, certainly can't be called a playmaker, because the space in which he operates is too restricted. In any case, defenders and defensive midfield players have become much tougher, wiser and faster than in the past. There is no longer enough space available for the free role that the inside-left used to have. That is why Hagi found it so difficult at Barcelona. The Ajax number 10 is usually Litmanen. He has to set an example by pressuring his opponent. Just compare that with the playmaker of 10 years ago! Today's playmakers are to be found in the center of the back four. This, of course, means that you can no longer deploy the old-fashioned, solid type of defender in these positions. You have to use technically and tactically gifted players like Blind and Rijkaard. The other defenders are also finding that they have to take a larger role in buildup play. Michael Reiziger, who is now playing for Barcelona, played right-half for FC Groningen before he came to Ajax. But he is quick, has good anticipation, learned how to play in a limited amount of space in midfield, and has sufficient ability to participate in buildup play. Initially his defensive play was not so good, but this is an aspect which can be taught quickly. I give a player like Reiziger more time to play himself into the team. It's not such a big gamble. We play near the center line, so Reiziger has time to use his basic speed to correct any mistakes he may make."

Restart plays

Van Gaal also has his own ideas about restart plays. For many months Ajax did not concede a single goal from a restart play. This, too, was clearly the consequence of a new concept.

"Before a game I often say that we can only lose games to opponents from restart plays. This automatically means that we have to be mentally alert to these situations and pay attention to detail. For example, I carefully analyze the characteristics of the opposing players who are strong in the air. Who prefers to go in powerfully, and who prefers to lie in wait? I then delegate the Ajax marker who is best suited to the relevant player's style.

The 'secret' of the free kick against us is that I put my trust completely in Van der Sar. I can still hit a good shot, but when I let fly at Van der Sar from 20 yards after a training session he holds almost every ball. So, if you think about it carefully, you have to create a situation on the field in which it comes down to the specialist versus Van der Sar. This means that, in contrast to other goalkeepers, Van der Sar never picks out one particular side of the goal. He always stands in the middle. Of course, he has to be able to see the ball through the defensive wall. We have found a way of ensuring that he can, but it cost us a lot of time. First you have to think the whole thing out, then you talk to Frans Hoek, the goalkeeper coach, and of course the rest of the coaching staff. Then you have to explain it to the whole group, discuss the pros and cons one by one, and practice it thoroughly in training.

The first few times we put the plan into execution in a real match, it almost rebounded on us. The players forgot to move aside at the right moment to create a gap for Van der Sar. However, you have to be brave enough to stick to your guns, and that is part of my character. You discuss it with the squad over and over again, and eventually the whole team is in favor of the situation. That's mainly down to communication. It's the same with corner kicks, from which we scored probably 20 goals two seasons ago. An important point in relation to this is that we've borrowed the principle of 'picking' from basketball. This means that, at the moment the corner is taken, Frank de Boer runs in the direction of one of the defenders marking the Ajax attackers and blocks him, with the result that a forward finds himself unmarked, especially because, more often than not, Frank's marker will also go with him.

But that's only one important detail of taking corners. You are always thinking about these situations. Players give you ideas. Frank de Boer suggested the idea of 'picking'. You're always on the look-out for creative solutions, and then you discuss them with the coaching staff and the players as well as trying them out in practice.

In this way you create the necessary support for innovations."

Chapter 3
The System

Almost every day, coaches travel from all over the world to Ajax's training facilities to try to fathom the secret of the Dutch club's success. These coaches stand along the sideline with their notebooks and write down the details of all of Van Gaal's drills. The Ajax coach has already said that these notes cannot shed any light on Ajax's secret. It is the whole approach, which you have to experience yourself - and, even then, with your own Ajax history as a basis - that gives an insight into the Amsterdam success formula. Blindly copying the Ajax style is therefore pointless. Nevertheless, we want to describe a few of the routine features of Ajax's play under the leadership of Louis van Gaal.

Possession

The most important characteristic of Ajax's game is that the team has so much possession. Possession is no guarantee of winning, but it has the great advantage that the opposition is forced to do a lot of running after the ball. By contrast, the Ajax players use much less energy, because they can allow the ball to circulate at speed (one or two-touch soccer) and keep their shape (lots of triangles on the field).

A significant statement by Louis van Gaal in this context: "Lots of coaches devote their time to wondering how they can ensure that their players are able to do a lot of running during a match. Ajax trains its players to run as little as possible on the field. That is why positional games are always central to Ajax's training sessions."

This starting point requires an excellent passing technique, and the ability to take the ball while facing the direction of play; the ball must also be played in at speed to the other members of the team. Important details, which can only be mastered by constant repetition during training and alert attention during the game. Or, as Lothar Mattheus said after the game in Vienna: "Ajax impressed me above all by their perfect passing, the fact that all their players are comfortable on the ball, and their perfect technique. That must be a question of training, training and more training. Always with the ball, as preached by the Ajax coaches. An example for the whole soccer world."

During the final in Vienna, even in the rather moderate first half Ajax succeeded in gaining 52% of the possession. For Ajax that is a relatively low figure, but many other clubs regard this as an important target to aim for.

Positional game

When Ajax is in possession, the players adopt a 3:4:3 formation. Under Van Gaal each position is linked to a fixed shirt number (see Figure 1), for the sake of clarity. In turn, each shirt number is associated with several basic tasks, which the player wearing the shirt has to carry out. There are tasks to be carried out when Ajax is in possession, and others to be carried out when the opposition has the ball. Ajax's youth teams play in the same manner, with the same tasks. This ensures the desired continuity.

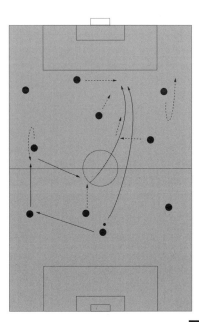

Ajax usually builds up its moves from the back. The goalkeeper only rarely kicks the ball long. Usually he plays it to one of the more creative defenders. It is noticeable that the whole team moves in set patterns. If one player comes back to make himself available to receive the ball, another makes a run towards the opposition's goal line.

The wide midfielders make a lot of forward runs, creating space for the long pass from the back to the advanced striker by pulling wide.

The same midfielders always remain behind their winger when he receives the ball, so that they do not curtail his action radius. The role of the midfielders is therefore always to support the strikers, and they must not overlap their wingers. That is a major departure from the tactics of Van Gaal's predecessors, who often allowed midfielders or even defenders to overlap down the flanks.

If an attack cannot be pursued down one flank, the task of the midfielders in Van Gaal's system is to ensure that the ball is switched to the other flank as quickly as possible.

Ajax almost always plays in a small area of the field in the opposition half. In this restricted space, good positional play and the ability to create space for others are of great importance for the team. This also applies to wing play. The two wingers stay wide to create space for the advanced central striker.

The favorite ploy is for the center forward to run into space, where he receives a long forward ball, which usually comes from the heart of the defense.

These are the broad outlines of the Ajax system in the Van Gaal era. We will now take a detailed look at each individual line of the team.

Defense

Ajax's defenders wear the numbers 2, 3, 4 and 5. The 2 and 5 are the fullbacks, and the 4 and 5 are the two players at the center of the defensive line.

Van Gaal's first priority for his full backs is that they play in a very disciplined manner. The strength of a player like Reiziger, for example, is his simplicity. When in possession he can play a faultless game, because he always chooses solutions that involve no risk of losing the ball. Preferably he will play the ball forward, but if he can't he will send it back to Van der Sar, who fulfills the role of the old fashioned sweeper, in that he is always available to take a pass when his team has possession. Van Gaal also expects his full backs to be so-called "killers," sticking to their task of marking their direct opponents out of the game with the utmost concentration.

Other "mandatory" characteristics are pure speed, tactical insight (being able to size up situations in advance and therefore knowing exactly when to close down space and cover colleagues), the ability to use both feet, and perfect passing technique.

The most obvious change that Van Gaal has introduced into the Ajax defensive line is at its center. Van Gaal does not select pure defenders to wear the 3 and 4 shirts. In fact the number 4 is the new playmaker. When the team is in possession, this is the player who has to join in the attack down the middle at the right moment, and make the decisive passes. When the opposition has possession he must have enough tactical insight to make the right choices; when to play in front of the defense, when to play alongside the number 3, and when to take up a position behind the other defenders. Together with the number 3, he must signal when pressing is to be carried out. He must also keep watch on the distances between the players who form the central backbone of the team and constantly give directions to the other players. It is clear that more than just defensive skills are needed for this role. This player must be able to contribute to the buildup and attacking play, but must also possess the same "killer" qualities as the full backs if the opposing team plays with three strikers and he then has to mark the opposing center forward.

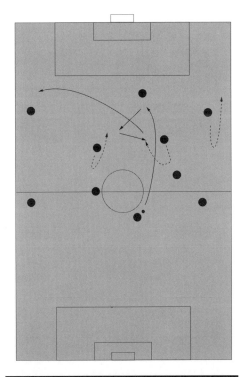 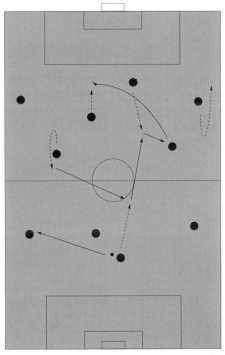

Midfield

In the Van Gaal system the right and left midfielders wear the numbers 6 and 8, and the central midfielder 10. Because the number 4 pushes up when the team has possession, the number 10 usually plays in advance of the other two midfielders. He is therefore the most important goalscorer in the central line. In his first years at Ajax, Van Gaal could play Bergkamp in this position. The Finn, Litmanen, then played there with considerable success. According to Van Gaal, Litmanen's tireless running and willingness to work for others make him so suitable for this central role in the Ajax system. When Ajax loses possession he immediately carries out his defensive tasks, and when Ajax is in possession he chooses the right moment to appear alongside his center forward as a second striker. The players on the right and left of the midfield line also have different tasks to fulfill under Van Gaal. Many coaches give these players a mainly holding role, but this is not enough for Van Gaal. He also expects his players to be able to make runs with the ball. Such runs can bring about a two against one situation, or open up enough space for the midfielder to try to score himself.

The skills of Ajax's wingers are such that they are often assigned two markers. The right and left midfielders can profit best from this, provided they have sufficient creativity and ball skills.

When the ball is lost, these midfielders must be able to gauge the situation and know exactly when and how to close down space. They must also have plenty of stamina, because they have to cover a lot of ground during the game.

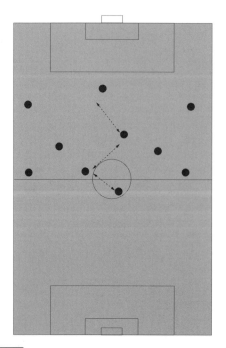 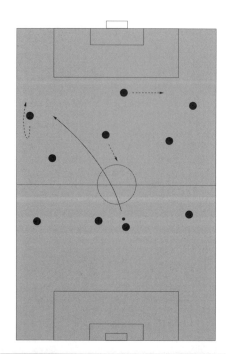

As has already been mentioned, the number 4 becomes the fourth midfielder when Ajax has possession. This player must therefore have many of the characteristics expected of the "genuine" midfielders, especially in the area of tactics.

It is a typical feature of the Ajax system that the players who make up the central backbone of the team are always in "echelon" during the buildup play (see Figure). The positions are then, by definition, well filled, and it is almost always possible to play in the "third man," who is released after a one-two.

Attack

The wingers are the numbers 7 and 11 in the Ajax system, with the center forward wearing 9.

There is always someone on the wings. The two wingers keep the playing area wide, thus making space for the center forward. Ajax's favorite play is to hit a long ball out of defense to the center forward, after he has moved into space (see Figure). The long ball forward usually comes from the heart of the defense. If this pass is not on, the ball is played to the feet of one of the wingers, whereby the midfielders first make forward runs and then stand ready to play a one-two with the winger. The winger must be able to read the game and to make the right choice: to make a run on goal, to cross the ball, to pass to a colleague, or to involve a third player in the exchange of passes. Obviously only a player with a perfect kicking technique can hit a perfect cross when under pressure.

Van Gaal introduced the most far-reaching change in the wingers' tasks at a very early stage. When the opposing team has the ball, the wingers now have to carry out much more defensive work. First of all they have to decide whether to exert pressure at once, or simply take up a defensive position. In the next phase, they have to provide cover and support in midfield. If possession is regained, they must race back to their original positions on the sideline in order to create space for their teammates.

Under Van Gaal, center forwards such as Stefan Pettersson and Ronald de Boer suddenly scored far fewer goals than, for example, Marco van Basten. Van Gaal's center forwards had other qualities. They were skilled at playing one-twos and creating space for their colleagues. Because Ajax plays in a small area of the field, the mobile midfielders and, in many cases, the defenders can cover the ground quickly to get into scoring positions. In exchanges of passes they frequently play the role of the so-called third man, who is played free after a one-two, partly as a result of the center forward's one-touch skills and ability to create space. Just as the fruits of this system were being harvested, however, a new young star emerged from Ajax's youth team. With Patrick Kluivert, Ajax suddenly had a center forward with good soccer skills who could also score regularly. This underlines the fact that every system is dependent not only on the coach's input but also on the players available.

Chapter 4
The Assistant Coach

In terms of character they are like chalk and cheese, but when it comes to soccer they could be Siamese twins. Louis van Gaal and his assistant, Gerard van der Lem. As assistant coach, Van der Lem is responsible for the final, most difficult transition faced by Ajax's talented young hopefuls - the step from the second eleven to the first team. Just as important is his role as a continuous sounding board for Van Gaal. Every week, they spend hours discussing even the tiniest details of practice drills, team selection, problems with the squad, or opponents. Knowledge imparts power, but Van der Lem never uses this in public. Although he sits next to Van Gaal on the bench during every match, and is consulted about substitutions, after the match he and Bobby Haarms retire to a quiet spot in the press room. Whisky in hand, he waves away questions. Comments are Van Gaal's prerogative, not Van der Lem's. He keeps his opinions for the coaches' meeting, which is held a day after the match. Who is this right-hand man, in whom Van Gaal has such blind faith?

At the age of 17 he ran out of the De Meer stadium, crying tears of rage and disappointment. After one conflict too many with Ajax's youth coach, the doors were finally closed against the talented but headstrong right winger. "Nothing will stop me from becoming a successful professional soccer player," vowed the young Van der Lem to himself just minutes later. And he kept his vow. As a colorful right winger, he played for FC Amsterdam, Roda JC, Feyenoord, Sparta and FC Utrecht. At this last club he was forced to retire on medical grounds. His knees were in such bad shape that professional soccer was no longer an option.

A career as a coach looked attractive. Like many coaches in professional soccer, Van der Lem first gained experience coaching young players - in his case at Haarlem, the club where Ruud Gullit started out on his breathtaking career. Three and a half years later, Van der Lem felt that he was ready to take over the job of chief coach, and the same Haarlem club gave him the opportunity.

However, in April 1990 he received a call from Leo Beenhakker, who was then the coach of Ajax. At first, Van der Lem thought that Beenhakker was calling to ask the price for Arthur Numan, an up and coming young star at Haarlem, who was later to play for the Dutch national team and to captain PSV Eindhoven. But Beenhakker was calling about Van der Lem himself, to ask whether he would consider becoming the Ajax youth coach for the 16 to 18 year olds and the 14 to 16 year-olds teams. Van der Lem, who was 37 at the time, did not rise to the bait immediately. Basically, he felt that a return to working with young players would be a step backward, even at Ajax, and he was not sure how he would get on with the youth coordinator, Louis van Gaal, who was known to have very distinctive ideas about soccer. The decision was made even more difficult for him, when other professional clubs offered him the job of chief coach.

Renewed discussion with Beenhakker followed, and Beenhakker managed to convince Van der Lem that working at Ajax could only further his development as a coach. Van der Lem insisted that Ajax should provide him with the opportunity to learn about every aspect of the club. He wanted to see how Beenhakker prepared the first eleven for top matches, how he handled star players, and how he planned the training sessions. When Beenhakker promised that Van der Lem would be regularly involved with the first eleven, the man from Amsterdam decided to sign a contract for two years. The many favorable reactions from fellow coaches soon reassured him that he had made the right choice.

In the early 1990s, the backroom staff of the Ajax youth development scheme consisted of Van der Lem, Ton Pronk, who was then still responsible for the second eleven and the Under 16 team, and Spitz Kohn, who coached the younger age groups. The overall leadership was in the hands of the coordinator, Louis van Gaal. At that time, the employment of four full-time coaches for youth development was unique in the Netherlands. The orders from the Ajax management left nothing to chance: talented Ajax players had to be ready for the first eleven at an early age. What the Spanish and Italians could do should be no problem for the Ajax club. The pressure on the youngsters had to be increased, and the demands on them had to be adjusted. On September 28, 1991, to the annoyance of everyone associated with Ajax, Leo Beenhakker resigned. Van Gaal took over the helm. During the first few matches, when it became obvious that the new coach's individual approach would not always result in wins, the fans yelled their displeasure from the bleachers, demanding the return of Johan Cruyff as chief coach. At this time, Van der Lem was already sitting next to Van Gaal in the dugout. The successful duo of Van Gaal and Van der Lem was born. The wind was soon to change, and would sweep them along to a veritable storm of success.

But success never comes of its own accord. From the moment that Van der Lem hit the trail with perfectionist Van Gaal, he realized that his life would never be the same again. Ajax was all that counted. His overcrowded working week bore testimony to this. The week started on Monday with the post mortem on the match played by the first eleven. Van der Lem then held a training session with the substitutes and reserve players. The afternoon was dedicated to the second eleven's match or a training session. Tuesday morning saw him back on the pitch with the first eleven, and the second eleven waited in the wings for its turn. On most Wednesdays the first eleven played a match. The program on Thursday was much the same as on Monday. Ajax's first team usually had Friday off, but Van der Lem held two training sessions with the second team. After coaching the first and second teams, Van der Lem often attended the matches played by the Under 18 team on Saturday. In the evening he would be on the bleachers to watch a professional soccer game, and on Sunday the first eleven played. Then there were the many work discussions, meetings, analyses of opponents in the European Cup competition, and scouting work. Yet Van der Lem thrived on this sort of pressure, to the extent that he no longer yearned for a job as a chief coach, which was his great ambition just a few years before. Most of all he looked forward to working abroad, a foreign adventure, with Van Gaal. His family will have some say in the matter. however, and the successful duo of Van der Lem and Van Gaal is not, according to Van der Lem, completely inseparable.

Drills

Van der Lem gets a tremendous kick out of the almost daily discussions with Van Gaal about practice drills.

"It is to the credit of the entire backroom staff at Ajax that no one can afford to be complacent or to rest on his laurels. The coaches take pains to keep each other on their toes. The principle is that everything that can be improved, must be improved. This is the bottom line for everyone.

Every step is recorded on paper and evaluated. After every weekend the match data (goals, assists, substitutions, cards, etc.) of all 176 players - from the first eleven to the youth teams - is entered into the computer. This data can be called up if any of the teams start to play below expectations.

The almost daily discussions about drills are another example of the constant struggle for perfection. Just take passing. According to the Ajax vision, this is an element which cannot be practiced enough. It is the most important instrument of team play. The passing drills are continuously adjusted to reflect the content of the latest discussions. In fact, compared with two years ago, this has led to a 100% improvement. The familiar triangles involving receiving the ball, playing the ball, and calling for the ball have become much more complex. For example, the player with the ball is always faced with two choices rather than one, because an extra player has been added. Faster reactions are then required. The player without the ball has to signal exactly what he wants at exactly the right moment. He must not do so too late, and certainly not too soon. When do you start your run, how hard do you hit the pass, and are you passing to the correct foot of the other player? Attention is constantly drawn to elements such as this. Coaching, monitoring and correcting, where necessary, ensure that the players remain sharp and alert.

Added to this we have the ideas of Van Geysel. He claims, on the basis of recent research data from the Free University, that the greatest benefit can be achieved by improving the speed of the first pass. Not only Jambor trains with this in mind. We also pay attention to this facet in the passing drills. Is the first pass hit hard enough to get away from the opposing players?

By dealing with this material every day, the players become very conscious of the subject and their reactions are heightened. This is reflected in interviews with Ajax players, who often refer in detail to the lessons of these training sessions.

From the Under 14s upward, Ajax training sessions are geared towards

5:3

Blind

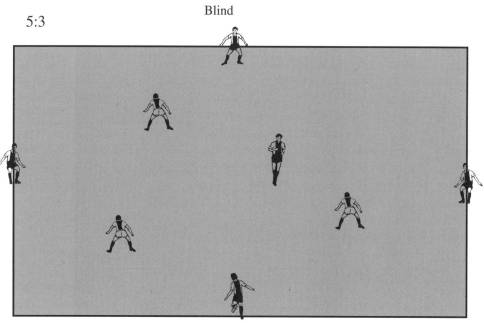

Frank de Boer

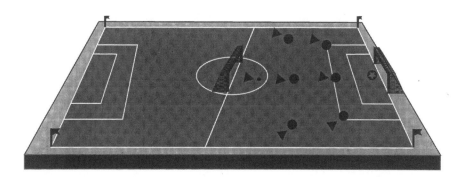

competitive games. This does not mean that every error made during a session is discussed. This would have a demotivating effect. Nor would it be correct, since each individual has to deal with the system as a whole, including his teammates and opponents. Individual shortcomings are only handled separately when technical skills are involved. During the many positional and small-team games, the players of the first eleven always play in their actual positions. This means that they receive individual coaching in a team context. "It is wonderful to be able to talk soccer in this way every day."

The following are a few examples of positional and small-team games used by Van Gaal and Van der Lem during Ajax's training sessions:

5:3 in a small rectangle (see diagram 1)

Frank de Boer and Danny Blind operate along the long sides of the rectangle, and the midfielders or backs on the short sides. The fifth player, Patrick Kluivert, is in the center. He may only touch the ball once, because that is what he has to do under match conditions. If Van Gaal calls for a game of 6:4, Litmanen and Kluivert, or other players who can play in the 9 or 10 position, stand between the four defenders. An interesting detail is that when Van Gaal took the Professional Soccer Course, he was failed on this drill because it was deemed "not related to a real soccer situation."

7:6 in half the pitch (see diagram 2)

Each player is in position. The team of seven has no goalkeeper in goal, and Blind is the sweeper. To prevent the team of six from scoring with a long shot into the empty goal, the team of seven has to pressure the ball constantly. This is only possible through excellent teamwork. It is also a drill whose form induces players to stay sharp and alert.

7:7 can be played for all manner of reasons

"Imagine that your team establishes a slight lead during a game, but then has difficulty retaining possession of the ball. The next day we play 7:7 with the rules adjusted accordingly. The team that scores first then has to keep possession for the next five minutes. Since this team may not score, the keeper of the other team can join in to ensure numerical superiority. In this way the pressure can be maintained on the player in possession.

I could give you many more examples. What is important is that a coach and a team have a specific concept. You need to know why you practice a specific drill. Only then can you decide the right time to use it."

The future

Van der Lem is the Ajax coach who works every day with the oldest group of talented young players. He has to be able to assess which of them will be able to move up to the highest level in the short term.

"Because a lot of Ajax's first-team players were injured in the 1996/97 season, quite a number of young players made their top level debuts earlier than planned. These include Arno Splinter, Dennis Schulp, Mario Melchiot, Rody Turpijn, Dave Van den Bergh, Robert Gehring, Menno Willems and Eli Louhenapessy. Sometimes they played well, and sometimes they were a disappointment. The second eleven also has a very young squad. John O'Brien is the first American contracted by Ajax, and is improving constantly. Jimmy Guy reminds me of Rijkaard, although such comparisons are dangerous. Kofey

Mensah and Milan Berck Beedenkamp are good defenders, and Luciano van Kallen is a typical Ajax right winger. But it is impossible to predict accurately who will get to the top eventually. The demands at the top are becoming harder. The most important thing is still how a talented young player handles the pressure, the expectations and, particularly, the disappointments. When Ajax sent me away at age 17, the coaches whose lives I had made difficult no doubt thought, 'Well, that is the end of Van der Lem in professional soccer. He will never make it.' So you see! Now I can use this example when, at the end of a season, I have to tell a young player that he is just not good enough for Ajax. Life at Ajax is wonderful. I whistle on my way to work every day. But there is life after Ajax, and what you make of it is largely up to you."

Chapter 5
The Search
for Talent

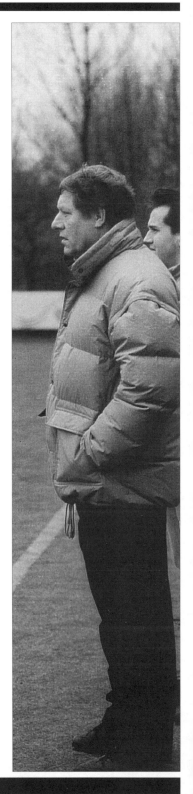

"What has been your major contribution to Ajax?" Louis van Gaal does not hesitate when asked this question. "Most people will consider it to be the way I have made Ajax play soccer, and the major successes we have achieved. Personally, I think that what was most significant was the way in which, during my first year with Ajax, I made crucial changes to the structure of the club. The club has been divided into two sections: the youth development section, and the professional soccer section. As director of the professional soccer section, I am responsible for the first eleven. In addition to myself, we have a director of the youth development section, in the person of Co Adriaanse. Ton Pronk has also become an important link within Ajax. Not only does he assist both Adriaanse and myself, but he is also the head scout, and is therefore the link between professional soccer and the youth development program. Ajax has a great deal to thank Ton Pronk for."

Who is Ton Pronk?

His main job is to scout for talented youngsters and to assess players already playing professionally, both at home and abroad. Ajax's player buying policy starts with him. He researches the qualities of these players in response to tips or his own observations. He works like a sort of secret agent, and this is a necessity, because as soon as word leaks out that Ajax is interested in a player, it becomes virtually impossible to buy him. The price goes up and competitors try to get in first. "Ajax 007", as he is called, scours the world in search of potential Ajax players.

Ton Pronk is so well known in the world of soccer that even his most innocent question causes concern. Obviously Pronk does all he can to gain information from the grapevine. He never does this directly, however, and he is used to taking roundabout routes.

"Everyone knows me and the work I do. For example, if I were to ask a journalist what he thinks about a certain soccer player, then his newspaper would probably publish a story that very day, stating that Ajax intends to buy the player in question. If we were interested in the player, we would then have no chance of getting him. So what I do is talk about a variety of soccer-related topics. Everybody knows everybody else in the soccer world, so it is all very relaxed. Discussions like this do not seem to be going anywhere in particular, but I very quietly and carefully steer them in the direction I want to go. Lots of things are talked about and, eventually, I get to hear what I have been listening for. As far as that is concerned, I am extremely inventive. When I tell Van Gaal some of the routes I have taken to gather information, he says: 'I don't know how you dare.' I have become adept at this kind of work. The trick is to get answers to questions you never asked.

The other trick is to let sleeping dogs lie for as long as possible. You have to use other channels to find out whether or not a player in whom Ajax is interested is playing. What sort of channels? That would be telling. They do not involve journalists, ex-players, etc., but people whose work or function puts them in a position of knowledge, without any link to Ajax being suspected. I have a number of people I can trust. People within the soccer world, who have a soft spot for Ajax. I regret that is all I can say on the subject. If I cannot get my information via the back door, then the front door is the only option left. For example, I might phone the office of the club in question directly, and pretend to be a journalist. In western Europe this poses a problem, but I can afford to take a chance with this approach in other parts of the world. The first and foremost rule is that I do not reveal my identity on first contact. Basically I try to maintain my anonymity for as long as possible. Once you have been recognized, you can go and sit openly in the stands. Until that time comes, I am simply another spectator, mostly seated opposite the main stand, where there is less chance of being recognized.

Because of Ajax's tremendous reputation, I am provided almost every day, in all manner of ways, with names of players who could be of interest to Ajax. Sometimes it is a phone call, and sometimes I find a note on my desk with just a name and a club. I prefer to keep my informers' names secret, but I always record the names of the players, in my head, in the computer, in a file. I check out what is known about the player in question. I have magazines and books, which are very useful when it comes to reviewing a past season. This method immediately supplies a wealth of information concerning most European competitions. If it then appears that Ajax suddenly needs a player in a specific position, I go through my files in search of a suitable candidate. These are mostly foreign players. Enough is known about the Dutch players. As soon as it has been ascertained - in the first place by Van Gaal - that there is no suitable Dutch player, we have to continue the search. Scouting assignments are formulated during the staff meetings held between Van Gaal, Adriaanse and myself every Monday afternoon. The less people who know that Ajax is interested in a specific player, the better. I am quite free to decide for myself whether to follow a lead. Although of course I consult Van Gaal."

Experience

During his career, Ton Pronk has assessed thousands of players on behalf of Ajax. He developed his keen eye for players who fulfill Ajax standards during his time as a player with Ajax himself. Between 1960 and 1970 Pronk played a total of 337 games for Ajax. He stopped when Rinus Michels started to restructure Ajax in the early 1970s, just before Cruyff's legendary Ajax started to dominate European soccer. Even so, in his last year with Ajax, Pronk played in a European Cup final. AC Milan proved too strong, however, and Ajax lost 1-4 at Real Madrid's famous Bernabeu stadium. The lanky defender completed his active career with FC Utrecht, before deciding to maintain his links with the soccer world as a coach. In 1976, Ajax coach Ivic asked Pronk how he felt about doing some scouting.

"Since that time, with the exception of my period as a coach for the amateur club Ijsselmeervogels, I have been a scout for Ajax, so I don't feel that I am boasting when I say that I possess sufficient experience. As a result, I can very quickly tell whether a player is good, average or bad, or one of the stages in between. Before you go to watch a player, you already know what position he will eventually have to play in. This means you already know what qualities this player must have. From the stands I take a good look at what he can do. If his performance is poor, I soon see this. I have a method of categorizing players. This makes it easier to explain things to Van Gaal. I say: 'He belongs to category this or that, but with a bit more of this and a bit less of that.' I am quick to judge. The player might not be involved in the game for the first half hour, so then I watch how he handles this, and whether it is his own fault. Reactions in these situations can be very revealing. In addition, the manner in which he moves also betrays a lot.

You could call it personality. What does he look like? This is my first priority. Based exclusively on appearance. Yes, even his hairstyle. It would be an exaggeration to say that I scout by hairstyle, but hair, clothing and general posture do give a first impression. If the first impression is a good one, you look further. Can he pass well? Has he got a good positional sense? Is he fast on the ball? Technical and tactical items. Finally, a complete report results, and it kindles enthusiasm or not, as the case may be. The problem of scouting for Ajax is the club's unique mode of play, which means that you have to assess whether a player's qualities will match a position within the Ajax system. This will always remain an unknown factor when it comes to buying players. This either has to be accepted, or Ajax will have to change its system of play, and that, to put it mildly, is not very likely. Not everyone fits into the system. This has been proved often enough. To the regret of Ajax and also, of course, to the regret of the players involved. This is why, whenever possible, it is a good idea to have players on trial for a while. Unfortunately, a contract has usually been signed before it becomes clear whether a player can fit into the Ajax pattern.

The most recent example of this is the Brazilian defender, Santos. He won the world championship with Brazil, but at Ajax he is kept out of the team by young players who have come through the club's own development system. Van Gaal justifies this by stating that the world champion does not fulfill the (constructive) demands within the stringent Ajax system."

Competition

"In this job it is not good to be too vain. You must be happy to remain anonymous, because that is how you can book the best results. I actually don't miss coaching, working with a group, at all. I thought it would cause me more problems, but I slipped into this specialized field of work so slowly that I now feel completely at home, and not because every day brings new adventures. My work does not consist exclusively of romantic, secret missions in foreign countries. It also involves youth scouting. And I get just as much satisfaction from sitting with 20 sets of parents watching an eight-year-old player in an Under 10 team, as from sitting in some foreign stadium among 90,000 spectators, watching some of the world's top stars. This is one of the reasons why I disagree with the repeated suggestion that more use should be made of ex-players. It is not difficult to enjoy exciting trips abroad, but in my opinion many of those who claim that Ajax makes too little use of them consider themselves too good to go and watch games at the Under 10 level. They are not concerned with Ajax's interests but only with their own status. They simply want to stand in the spotlight."

The huge rise in players' salaries in recent years has not made the search for top foreign players easier.

"It is a hard, hard world. Fortunately not all my colleagues are ruthless types. There are still some hopeless bunglers. For example, in Norway I saw a group strolling about arrogantly in their club colors, but I soon noticed that they made a wide detour around the executive offices, because they were supposed to be 'incognito'. And I am talking about a top European club. Which one? No, I won't tell. My competitors are getting tougher all the time, that is a fact. At the same time, this is a challenge. I have to do my work more and more circumspectly, be more and more discreet. Without losing sight of my own standards and values."

"Ajax 007" says that he is not troubled by paranoia. The fact that names are omitted in his telephone conversations with Van Gaal is, according to him, just a sensible precaution.

"I love my job. Mainly because I hope that I can contribute to the future success of my club, Ajax. I can only do this job for this club, because this is where my heart is." It is this attitude and his impressive know-how which generate the respect with which the amiable Pronk is viewed at Ajax.

Chapter 6
The Goalkeeping Specialist - Frans Hoek

In the words of Johan Cruyff: "As the coach of a top club, you cannot possibly be an expert at everything. The trick is to collect a team of the best possible specialists around you, to help with matters you know little about." This idea was put into practice by Van Gaal at Ajax. It also applies to the support and coaching of goalkeepers.

At Ajax this is the province of Frans Hoek. During his career, Hoek fell just short of the very top, but he did play in the first division for many years with FC Volendam. After the end of his active career, goalkeeping remained the key to success for Hoek. He learned to stand up for himself during a none too easy youth, and as an adult coach he translates this characteristic into tremendous enthusiasm and striving for perfection. Frans Hoek is also one of the first goalkeepers ever to analyze the goalkeeper's job in minute detail. He was quick to set this genuine know-how down on paper. His coaching videos have become the international bible for every coach who works with goalkeepers. Whether we are talking about a professional club, an amateur team or a youth team.

The next step was to organize training camps, where goalkeepers and their coaches could be trained. Stanley Menzo was then the Ajax goalkeeper. Hoek has a very special bond with this young goalkeeper from Surinam. For a long time, Menzo was the embodiment of all of Hoek's theories on the modern goalkeeper. Menzo saw his goalkeeper coach as the absolute expert, the man who could take him from his underdog position to the very top. It must have been a very difficult moment for both of these top athletes when Van Gaal gave preference to Van der Sar as first-choice goalkeeper. Always the professional, Hoek took up his work with Van der Sar. In no time at all, the lanky goalkeeper became the best goalkeeper in the Netherlands, was selected for the Dutch national team, and is today thought by many to be the top goalkeeper in the world. Menzo was forced to continue his career elsewhere, with Ajax's arch rival PSV. When PSV chose the quirky Waterreus in preference to him, Menzo fled across the border to Belgium, where he became the first-choice goalkeeper for Eric Gerets' Lierse SK.

Although Menzo's career may have hit a downward spiral, his teacher, Frans Hoek, continued to flourish. His video projects achieved great success. His expertise, natural charisma and his gift of getting his message over in a professional manner made him a welcome lecturer at demonstration sessions all over the world. Hoek opened his own store near Amsterdam, selling equipment for coaches and goalkeepers. He also developed special goalkeeping courses in conjunction with the KNVB.

But his main job is still training goalkeepers at Ajax, for both the first team and the youth teams. When he is not busy with other work or commitments, Frans Hoek can be found in the dug-out during first team matches. He then focuses all his attention on goalkeeper Edwin van der Sar. After each match he prepares a detailed analysis of how Van der Sar played. In line with the principles of the Van Gaal school, this is talked through in a dialogue rather than presented as a monologue.

European Cup Final

The preparations for the second final in the Champions League during the Van Gaal era are a good example of the way he works. This is the story of an expert driven by passion.

"The preparations for the important final game against Juventus started on 15 May 1996. First of all we looked at the initial situation. As far as the goalkeepers were concerned, Ajax was in an ideal situation. Van der Sar could look back on an excellent season. He was physically fit, had suffered no injuries, and a week's vacation had made him mentally fit to meet the new challenge. During this period the second goalkeeper, Fred Grim, trained with the second team, and he was both physically fit and in form.

On the road to a match as important as the Champions League final, goalkeeper coaching has two objectives: general preparation, and specific training, which takes account of the characteristics of the opposing team."

Checklist

"When you put together the practice drills for the general preparation, you have to look at the demands that are made on goalkeepers in a match of this importance. If you do this critically and carefully, a sort of checklist will emerge of its own volition. You take account of what types of ball the goalkeeper will have to deal with, such as long balls, crosses, shots, headers, one-to-one duels, and back passes. At the same time, you try to vary distances and positions as much as possible, as well as the way the ball approaches: low, high, bouncing, from a volley or a drop-kick, inswinging, outswinging, or hanging in the air.

You also include all types of game situations in the drill, including restarts by the opposition. It is also essential to pay attention to the goalkeeper's role when he is in possession, i.e. to his part in the build-up. In this context, we look at the choice between a fast release of the ball or a slow one, taking lots of time for a throw out, a kick from the hands, a kick from a back pass or, for example, a goal kick or a free kick."

Analysis of Juventus

"Obviously your checklist for the drills geared to the next opponent is always based on the match analyses. In the weeks before the match, the Ajax backroom staff analyzed Juventus in detail. As the goalkeeper coach, I personally took a critical look at key summaries of Juventus's games. From these I reached the following important conclusions about Juventus.

• Van der Sar could expect to face shots from all angles and at any time from in front of the goal from Vialli (right-footed but can use the left) and Ravanelli (left-footed but can use the right), and from the attacking midfielders.

• Most attacks would be built up down the flanks. Crosses from the left would often be made right-footed, as would crosses from the right. The crosses would be hit hard, either inswinging or outswinging, and would be aimed between the goalkeeper and the incoming attackers, who nearly always take up position in echelon. The build-up would sometimes be through the middle, with Juventus trying to create a scoring chance quickly. An important general characteristic would be the high tempo of the moves, and the often opportunistic approach.

Restart plays:

"In general, Juventus had a good record of scoring either directly or indirectly from restart plays that season, and we knew that a lot of time was devoted to practicing these situations.

• Corners would nearly always be taken by the right-footed Del Piero, i.e. inswinging from the left and outswinging from the right.

• Free kicks to the left of the goal would also be taken by Del Piero with his right foot, with great precision and high speed, towards the near or the far post (the majority toward the near post, depending to some extent on the position of the goalkeeper).

Further to the right of the goal, free kicks would more usually be taken by Padovano, Yugovic, Conte, etc. These would be hit hard and straight at the goal, either directly or after a pass from a teammate.

• The penalty specialist was Ravanelli. As a left-footed player he takes penalties in two ways: the "Neeskens penalty", blasted at the middle of the goal, or a placed shot to the right of the goalkeeper.

At this level, even the type of ball used in a match is relevant. In the final this would be an Adidas Questra, with its specific characteristics. We trained with these balls from the very start."

Training drills

"When you plan training sessions, you must realize that physical conditioning is stimulated by a combination of the intensity of the drill, the number of repetitions, and a good ratio of work to rest periods.

If you work with two goalkeepers like Van der Sar and Grim, one keeps goal and the other acts as a 'server'. Both must be aware that they have to train as though playing in a genuine game, handling the ball and making the choices they are faced with in a real match. During a training session, they must therefore avoid making any uncharacteristic moves, due to tiredness or the speed of execution.

Obviously the goalkeepers change over regularly. Sometimes the changeover is signaled in advance. But naturally you observe them continuously during the session, and the goalkeepers often decide for themselves when to make the change.

A final general comment is that, during the preparations for the match against Juventus, muscle strengthening exercises, particularly for the stomach, back and arm muscles were part of the program. These were repeated continually."

15 May

At 10.45 a.m., on 15 May, in the De Meer stadium, Ajax started the first training session that was fully geared to the important confrontation with Juventus. After the whole squad had warmed up without the ball, the two goalkeepers went to train separately. At that moment the drills were aimed at general preparation.

Frans Hoek and goalkeeper 2 (this is always the 'server' goalkeeper) took turns kicking the ball within reach of goalkeeper 1 (the 'genuine' goalkeeper), who stopped the balls and returned them. Obviously, positions were constantly changed, and both 'strikers' used their perfect kicking technique to vary the types of ball (e.g. kicking with the inside or the outside of the foot; with and without spin; volley or instep) and the speed of the ball.

The two then played back passes to goalkeeper 1, who sent the ball back into play again. Here again, the positions changed constantly, and the level of difficulty of the balls played in was varied.

In the third training situation, Frans Hoek kicked the ball towards goalkeeper 1, who dealt with it and sent it towards goalkeeper 2, who dealt with it in turn. Goalkeeper 1 dealt with the ball both as a back pass and as a ball coming from the opposition. He returned it into play with a drop kick, a volley or a throw.

In the next drill goalkeeper 1 had to take the incoming ball diving (lying) sideways, and then throw it back to goalkeeper 2. The number of shots at goal varied between 4 and 12. There were also different ways of shooting: high or low, inswinging or outswinging, varying the ball speed and the speed of play. In the latter case, in each situation the goalkeeper might or might not be allowed to get back into position before a new shot was taken.

In the fifth and last drill, Frans Hoek played the balls alternately (left and right) to the goalkeeper, who dealt with them as fast as possible. The drill was repeated three times, with four to six balls per drill.

This training session was rounded off with a 5 v 5 small sided game with two goalkeepers.

In order to ensure that the players were sharp and alert, the rule was: when the ball is out of play, the player who gets to it first can throw it in. Ajax calls this drill 'First come, first served!'. When a corner is taken, play is quickly restarted by the goalkeeper of the team entitled to the corner.

Frans Hoek: "This type of exacting play in a restricted space is ideal for the goalkeeper. He is faced with everything that could happen during a real game. The adapted rules of play improve the desired sharpness and alertness to optimal level."

1

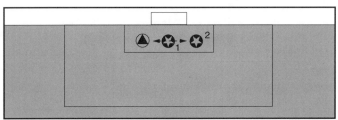

2

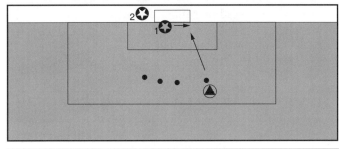

3

4

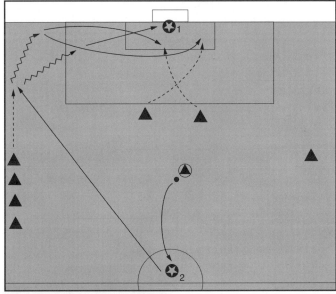

16 May

The second training session took place between 10.30 and 11.45 on Thursday, 16 May, in the De Meer stadium. Once more the goalkeepers trained separately, after the general warming up without the ball had been completed. This time interval training was on the program, based on a work to rest ratio of 1:2, followed by 1:1.

The work was carried out in two series, structured as follows:

Series 1:
5 seconds of work - 10 seconds of rest
10 seconds of work - 20 seconds of rest (2x)
5 seconds of work - 10 seconds of rest

Series 2
5 seconds of work - 5 seconds of rest
10 seconds of work - 10 seconds of rest (2x)
5 seconds of work - 5 seconds of rest

The training session started with the same drills as on the previous day. In the second drill, the interval scheme was used for the first time. Frans Hoek and goalkeeper 2 stood ready in a marked area, with a ball between their hands. At a signal, goalkeeper 1 moved continuously between goalkeeper 2 and Frans Hoek, alternately touching the back of the ball with one hand: right to right and left to left. The distance between the coach and the goalkeeper changed, as did the height at which the ball was held (see diagram 1).

In the following drill, Frans Hoek played one ball after another into a marked area. Goalkeeper 1 defended this area and dealt with all balls as back passes, which he then played to goalkeeper 2 (see diagram 2). The interval scheme was used again.

The same applied to the following drill. From various positions Frans Hoek kicked the ball to the near or the far post. Goalkeeper 1 tapped the hand of goalkeeper 2 and dealt with the ball again and again (see diagram 3). The shots varied in terms of difficulty and speed.

This lively drill was rounded off with a "system" exercise, in which both goalkeepers were deployed (see diagram 4).

A coach played the ball to the goalkeeper, who played it to the player who was calling for it on his left, who:

a. dribbled in and shot at goal;

b. dribbled to the goal line and crossed to the incoming strikers or

c. cut inside and hit a right-footed cross between the goalkeeper and the incoming strikers.

If the ball was played out to the right, Finidi crossed to the incoming strikers. Goalkeeper 1 dealt with the ball and sent it out to goalkeeper 2 when he had possession.

Players on the left: Hoekstra, Wooter, Musampa and Van de Bergh
Player on the right: Finidi
Strikers: Litmanen and Kanu

5

6

7

8

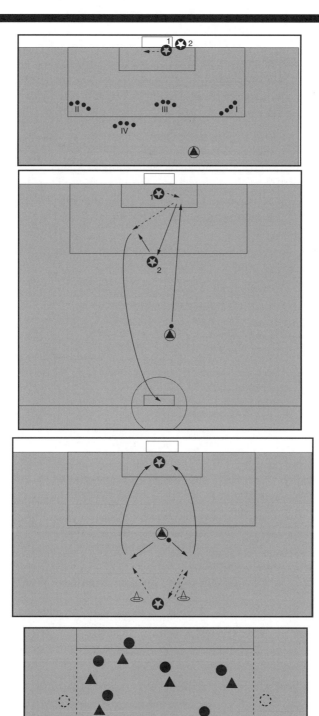

17 May

Two training sessions were held on Friday, 17 May. The program from 10.30 to 11.45 involved warming up without the ball by the entire group, a 6 v 6 heading drill with two goals and two goalkeepers (small pitch), and a 3 v 3 'sharp' competitive game with two goalkeepers (small pitch). Van der Sar received a painful knee injury during the latter game.

The second training session took place between 17.00 and 18.15. After the familiar group warming up without the ball, the goalkeepers again trained separately. The first drill was the same as on 15 and 16 May. Then Frans Hoek shot a series of balls, 2 x 4, 2 x 5, and 2 x 6, to the right and left of the goalkeeper, who saved them. Ball speed, trajectory, shooting distance and angle, as well as the moment of play, were varied.

The goalkeeping coach then took shots at the open part of the goal from various positions (see diagram 5) and in various ways. Goalkeeper 1 tagged goalkeeper 2 before saving the ball. Fred Grim then joined the full squad to act as a goalkeeper in a 7 v 6 game. Frans Hoek continued with Van der Sar. The subsequent drill was based on the analysis of Juventus. Hoek played an outswinging cross from the sideline between Van der Sar and the cone on the penalty spot. When Van der Sar was troubled by his knee, he was allowed to rest after consultation. Hoek and Van der Sar used the time to discuss Juventus. The training session finished with a small sided game of 6 v 6.

18 May

On Saturday, 18 May, training was resumed. The whole group warmed up without the ball, then came the familiar first drill, when the goalkeepers were coached separately. Frans Hoek then played the ball to goalkeeper 1, who played it to goalkeeper 2. He played the ball back to goalkeeper 1, who was calling for it (right or left), who then played it towards the empty goal (see diagram 6). There are a host of possibilities even in such a relatively simple drill. Just think of the ways in which the ball can be played, either directly or after controlling it, consciously playing to a specific foot, or the kicking technique used for shooting. The goalkeepers changed over after each series of 4 to 8 balls.

In the third drill, Hoek played the balls alternately to the left and to the right. Goalkeeper 1 shot alternately left-footed and right-footed at goal. Goalkeeper 2 defended the goal and saved the shots.

In the fourth drill, Hoek played the balls between the goalkeepers. Goalkeeper 2 was a passive opponent. Goalkeeper 1 dealt with the ball and directed it towards the empty goal. Here again, the drill was repeated in a series using 3 to 6 balls.The fifth drill was actually a repeat of drill 3, except that goalkeeper 1 had to go back to a line between two cones (see diagram 7).The sixth drill was the same as the fourth drill. This time the goalkeeper had to send the

9

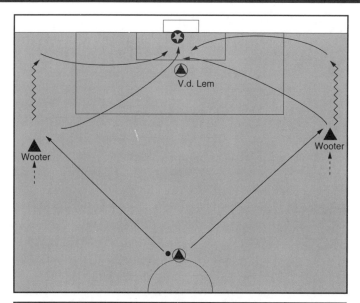

10

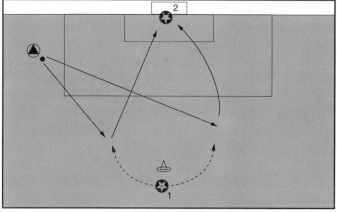

11

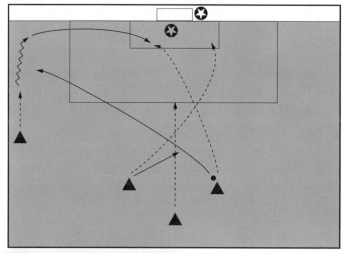

ball back into play with a powerful kick (fast and far) towards the opposing goal.

The session was finished off with a small sided game of 6 v 6, with the target players on the goal line at first, and then on the sideline (see diagram 8).

An additional, extremely difficult challenge for the goalkeepers was to try to intercept the pass to the target players on the goal line or on the sideline on the right.

20 May

On Monday 20 May the final training session was held in Amsterdam. After the usual quarter of an hour warming up, the goalkeepers again left the main group.

The two traditional starting drills took on a significant new aspect. The shots from Frans Hoek and goalkeeper 2 were no longer deliberately kicked within reach of goalkeeper 1. From the word go, the emphasis was on scoring. In the first drill, the shots came from outside the penalty area, and in the second, from inside it.

In the third drill, Frans Hoek shot from outside the penalty area from the second line, at the goal defended by goalkeeper 1. Goalkeeper 2 stood at a distance of 5 to 8 yards in the path of the shot. He could touch the incoming ball or, if goalkeeper 1 could not hold it (within the penalty area), he could deal with the rebound. Subsequently Fred Grim went to keep goal in a 7 v 6 drill.

Edwin van der Sar remained together with Nordin Wooter and Gerard van der Lem. Frans Hoek played the ball to Wooter who, after controlling it, could dribble before making an early cross, before reaching the goal line, aimed between the goalkeeper and the opponent, Gerard van der Lem, (see diagram 9).

After one series, the ball was played to Wooter on the other side. Wooter cut inside and played the ball between the goalkeeper and the opponent with his right foot. Finally Wooter took the ball to the goal line and crossed it in front of goal.

In the following drill, Van der Sar was replaced by Grim and Wooter by Blind. Grim played the ball to Blind, who, after controlling it, passed to one of the coaches on the right or left side. When the coach received the ball, he crossed it early to Grim, between Grim and the penalty spot. Grim caught the ball and sent it back into play.

21 May

On Tuesday, 21 May, the first training session held on Italian soil, between 11.00 and 12.15, at the AS Roma training complex in Trigoria.

The first, familiar drill started with scoring attempts from inside the penalty area. In the second drill, goalkeeper 1 played the ball to the coach, who played it back to the right or the left. Goalkeeper 1 sent the ball to goalkeeper 2, who again played it to the coach. The goalkeepers had to make choices: whether to control the ball, whether to dribble or not, or to play the ball directly, one touch. The distance from the sideline was also varied.

The third drill was familiar: the coach crossed the ball, goalkeeper 1 dealt with it, then played it towards goalkeeper 2, who also dealt with it. The various methods of crossing, taking the ball, and returning it into play have already been described in the earlier part of this chapter.

In the fourth drill Frans Hoek and goalkeeper 2 took turns in trying to score against goalkeeper 1, who was given the opportunity to take up his position each time.

In the fifth drill, Frans Hoek played the ball to goalkeeper 1, who then took it round the cone. Goalkeeper 1 shot at the goal. Goalkeeper 2 defended his goal, and saved the ball (see diagram 10). After a series of 4 to 6 balls, a changeover was made.

In the sixth drill, goalkeeper 1 tagged the coach and kicked the ball, via a goal kick, toward goalkeeper 2, who kept changing position. In a series of 4 to 8 balls, the goal kicks were taken alternately with the right and the left foot, hard and direct, or high into the air.

The seventh drill was a repeat of drill 3 on 20 May.

Winston Bogarde and Gerard van der Lem took part in the eighth and final drill.

From the sideline, Frans Hoek and Grim hit inswinging and outswinging crosses aimed between Van der Sar, Bogarde and the opponent, Gerard van der Lem. This drill concentrated on the cooperation between Bogarde and Van der Sar: communication, dealing with the ball and reciprocal back up.

The final training session was held from 20.00 to 21.15 on the same day, in the Olympic Stadium in Rome. Jari Litmanen was in charge of the warming up. The goalkeepers trained separately. The drill focused on the now familiar method of dealing with back passes and crosses, and returning the ball into play when in possession. After these drills, the coaches decided to change goals. Nothing was left to chance. A number of training drills were practiced, relating to an attack down the wings, with incoming strikers (see the example in diagram 11). Resistance was at first passive, then full. The drill finished without the resistance of the opponents. Finally Van der Sar had to handle a variety of balls from the edge of the penalty area.

The final

The day of the final arrived. Ajax made a mediocre start. To everyone's surprise, even Edwin van der Sar looked nervous and insecure in goal during the first half hour. Unusually he failed to play free balls accurately to his teammates, did not communicate adequately with the defenders, appeared to be uncomfortable when receiving back passes, and dropped a shot. Ravanelli seized the opportunity. After this bad start, Van der Sar pulled himself together, as only a top class goalkeeper can under these circumstances. His excellent positional play, good reflexes and calm handling of the ball drew attention. When the deciding penalties came, he guessed the correct corner four times.

"Even if I look very critically at the final, I cannot conclude that we did not do everything possible to prepare Van der Sar optimally for the duel. There were no surprises. This is why I have no explanation for the weak start. Everything we saw during the match had been dealt with during the preparation. All playing situations, restarts, the tactics, etc. Everything had been discussed and trained for. The only unknown factor was who, apart from Ravanelli (and Vialli), would take the penalties, and how. Edwin and I, therefore, discussed this before the penalty shoot-out began. During the game I had analyzed the player "types." We came to the conclusion that the tough, hard players would most probably shoot hard to the same side as their favored foot, i.e. right-footed players would shoot to the left of the goalkeeper, and left footed players to the right. This is what actually happened four times, and Van der Sar was close each time. The Italians took the penalties perfectly, however, and he had no chance. If the more technical players such as Del Piero and Deschamps had had to take penalties, they would probably have waited longer to see what the goalkeeper was going to do. You have to be able to handle this as well. Top matches are, after all, decided by details."

But even specialist Frans Hoek has no answer to the question of why Ajax goalkeeper Van der Sar was not himself during the first half hour. Unfortunately, even the most perfect of preparations cannot take away the unforeseeable moments in a match.

Chapter 7
Assistant Coach Bobby Haarms

For as long as anyone can remember, he has been active as assistant coach for the club he loves: Ajax. In 1996 Bobby Haarms celebrated his 25th anniversary as an Ajax coach - a unique achievement. Throughout that time he put his own club, where he played as an amateur and then as a professional, before lucrative offers from elsewhere. Bobby Haarms epitomizes loyalty to a single club. He was assistant to, in succession, Rinus Michels, Stefan Kovacs, George Knobel, Hans Kraay, Michels again, Tomaslav Ivic, Cor Brom, Leo Beenhakker, Johan

Cruyff, Beenhakker again, and Louis van Gaal. Haarms still puts loyalty to his chief coach as one of his main priorities.

He could never become chief coach, except for a few interim periods, because he never found the time to acquire the top Dutch coaching diploma. When the opportunity arose, Michels had need of him and Bobby withdrew from the course. To the annoyance and dismay of the course director, who was convinced that he had made the wrong choice. Be that as it may, Haarms has never regretted his decision. It has made him the most famous assistant coach in the Dutch soccer world.

On one occasion, he was told that he was no longer needed. That was in 1981, when Kurt Lindner was appointed coach for the first time. Suddenly the club's board of management found that Haarms was surplus to requirements as assistant coach and gave him the job of scout instead. He was unhappy in his new job, and felt out of place watching minor level games in remote towns and villages, where there were perhaps only 20 spectators, all of them asking each other in loud whispers what Haarms was doing there. He could not get used to his new role, and often thought of the time when Rinus Michels waited for him with his wife Wil at Schiphol Airport, after he had been abroad for the first time to look for a new striker. So he resigned, and didn't return until 1986, when Cruyff asked him to take over the post of youth coach at Ajax. Since then he has been a permanent fixture. Down the years, Haarms has become a respected figure at Ajax, not just for his loyalty, but for his skills as a coach and above all as a "rehabilitation trainer." Haarms has his own methods of helping injured players back to the level of fitness needed to rejoin the squad.

The route back

An injured player's route back to fitness starts when he leaves the operating room. First of all he goes to physiotherapist Pim van Dord, then to conditioning trainer Laszlo Jambor. The final obstacle to be overcome before he can rejoin the first-team squad is Bobby Haarms. With a mixture of fear and respect, the players undergo a series of tough training sessions. When they can complete them all without feeling any discomfort from their injury, they are ready to rejoin the squad. This marks the end of a lonely period, during which the affected player looks longingly at the squad training sessions. Injured players are not left to their own devices at Ajax, but they have to carry out most of their work on their own during this time.

Haarms:"The field is empty, and we two go out into the rain. Often in winter you can see your breath rise up in front of you like smoke in the early morning air. And, of course, they have gone through a difficult time. The treatments meted out by Van Dord are no joke, nor is the conditioning training with Laszlo Jambor, and only absolutely fit players can make it through the time they spend with me."

Drills

"The training session begins with warming-up. The muscles have to be prepared for the coming exertion, and the player also needs to get into the right state of mind. Most of them know what is coming, and that it won't be easy. They must be physically prepared, but getting in the right frame of mind is perhaps even more important.

The sessions are carried out from start to finish with a ball. Most of the things you do without a ball are mind-numbing. The ball also distracts the player's attention from his injury. He has to think about the ball, not the injury. Moreover, a player is always hungry for the ball after an injury period. He has not been able to touch a ball, and the moment when he can do so again is the first milestone on the way back. He looks forward to it, even though he knows that he is going to suffer and that he will have to get through a lot of hard work. He enjoys just having a ball at his feet again.

The warming-up exercises that I carry out with them together always start very calmly.

1. First, I throw the ball alternately to the player's right and left foot, and the player has to side-foot the ball back into my hands while running on the spot. Depending on the stage of the player's recovery, the number of times this is repeated can be steadily increased to 20.

2. This is followed by running on the spot and making a small jump to head the ball back when I throw it.

3. Then comes kicking the ball back with the instep, right and left. During the first series of about 20 repeats the ball is thrown high, so that the knee has to be drawn up high.

4. Then I run a little way backward, so that the ball is thrown a little lower and the player is forced to kick the ball low with the instep. This is a little harder, which is why the high kicks are carried out first. If this exercise goes well, you can continue.

5. The sideways movement is introduced. The player moves from left to right and heads the ball into my hands.

6. The ball is side-footed back as the player moves sideways. This exercise also tests the hip joint.

7. Throw the ball up, catch it on the chest, and play it back left and right.

8. The player stands with his back to me, calls "yes" and turns alternately over his right and left shoulders to head the thrown ball back into my hands.

This exercise ends the warming up. The above exercises are designed to warm up the muscles and to test whether the player can perform the basic movements.

9. Six balls are laid next to each other on the edge of the penalty area. The player has to kick the balls to the center line and then kick them from the center line into the penalty area at the other end of the field. He must ensure that the balls are as close together as possible near the center line, so that he does not have to cover too much ground when he kicks them into the other penalty area. Soccer players do not like running, so they automatically do their best to achieve this. After all six balls have been kicked for a second time, the player runs at about 75% of his full speed to the penalty area where the balls are now located. At first the player has to side-foot the balls, but from the second or third day he can use his instep. In the starting phase I do this twice; once upfield and then once back again. This means that the player kicks the ball 24 times from the ground.

A series of exercises is then carried out on the "Swedish bench". This is a wooden bench, which is also present in a more modern form in gymnasiums.

10. On the first day the player stands astride the bench and has to touch the top of the bench thirty times alternately with right and left foot. This number is increased day by day.

11. The player faces along the bench, with one foot on each side of it, and jumps onto the bench with both feet 20 times.

12. Also facing along the bench, the player jumps 30 times over the bench, alternating left and right, whereby the other foot is placed on the bench.

13. At the end of the bench session, the player jumps two-foot over the bench, from left to right, with an intermediate hop.
The number of times each exercise is carried out is increased by 10 each day, to a maximum of 50 or 60.

It is important that the player rests between each exercise. He then runs 20 yards, turns, and runs back 20 yards to loosen up his legs. The muscles need to become accustomed to the exercises. I watch the players while they are running. I look to see how they run, and whether they are tired. During the rehabilitation training the player's basic condition must also be honed. When players come back after a long injury period, they obviously need time to get back into condition. They will already have worked with the conditioning trainer, Laszlo Jambor, but they will not yet be back to their old level. In fact they will not reach it until they have trained a few times with the whole squad and can hold their own in positional games without difficulty.

The Swedish bench is followed by the board.

14. The player stands about a yard from the board and side-foots the ball against it, using his right and left feet alternately. The pace is automatically fairly high, and it is also important to take an intermediate step before each ball contact. The first time there are 40 repeats, and this number is increased by 20 each time. I once got up to 200 with one player. It is a good exercise for improving the player's feeling for the ball, as well as his concentration. Ultimately the player becomes tired, and his ball control sometimes suffers. I always have an extra ball within reach, so the player can continue at the same tempo if the first ball bounces away.

15. The exercise is carried out again, but this time the ball is kicked with the instep.

Finally the player can shoot at the goal.

16. At the edge of the penalty area the player runs on the spot. I stand on the sideline and roll the ball 10 times to his healthy side and 10 times to the other. This drill sharpens up a player's timing. At first Winston Bogarde had a few problems with the exercise. I let him practice frequently, because the most important thing is not how often the drill is repeated but how well it is carried out. Each drill is a combination of strength, skill, concentration, suppleness and condition.

What you often see is that a player is not troubled so much by the injury but by other muscles or joints. That can happen if he is still favoring the injury, and therefore carries out more work with other parts of the body to compensate for this.

17. Then comes quick-fire shooting. At the edge of the penalty area, 10 balls lie close to each other. The player has to work his way at speed along the line, moving from inside to outside, shooting at goal with the inside of the foot. Here too, he can use his good foot first and then the other.

18. I then take 10 balls and I go and stand behind the goal. The player runs up from the penalty spot and I throw a ball over the goal. The player jumps, heads the ball at goal, then sprints round the cone. And so on. I vary the height.

19. This is really the same exercise, but this time with shooting instead of heading. The player has to shoot with the instep, alternately right and left, both 5 times. The player volleys the ball as it falls, then he sprints round the cone. All at a high speed. I switch exercises 18 and 19 every two times.

20. From the third or fourth day there is another shooting drill. 10 balls are placed on the edge of the penalty area, with 5 of them on the right and 5 on the left, and a small gap in between. I stand about 3 yards behind. The player always shoots the innermost balls at goal, turns, sprints to me, "tags" me, and then turns to kick the next ball. Two series follow.

21. The player then goes and stands on the line. I play the ball along the ground to him. The player runs in and taps the ball back, then runs backward at full speed. This is a typical "ta-ta-ta" drill, whereby I

call and clap my hands in the tempo of the sprint. It is also important for the trainer to encourage and "drive" the player during each drill. He has to hear, feel and know that you are involved with heart and soul. It is also 90 minutes of concentration and effort for me. We do it together. When we finish I am often sweating just as much as the player, and I am just as exhausted. Of course, you can tell the player to carry out a drill and then just fold your arms and stand watching in silence until he is finished, but that does not work. Such a youngster has a lot to swallow. He wants to get back into the squad as soon as possible. Probably so that he can get away from me, and also because that is where it all happens. And if I demand 100 percent effort, then I also have to give 100 percent myself.

22. Almost at the end he is given a ball and then I tell him, "The field is yours. Do what you want." Then he has to race over the field for 30 seconds. Relatively calmly at the start of the recovery period, but later at full speed. The emphasis is on speed, stopping, turning, swerving and making feints. After 30 seconds he can rest, and he is then allowed to say when he is ready to start again. At first he will sometimes hold back, because he is not sure what he can and cannot do, but gradually you see him forget his early injury-related limitations and he will try to do the most amazing things. And this boosts his self-confidence.

23. Finally there are the 6 cones, which are positioned in the shape of a boat.
(The distance between two cones is always about 20 yards.)

23a: AB walk - BC dribble - CD sprint - DE walk - EF dribble - FA sprint.

23b: AB walk - BC dribble - CD sprint, there and back - CD walk - DE walk - EF dribble - FA sprint, there and back.

23c: Same as 1, until CD: sprint there, back and back again - FA sprint there, back and back again.

23d: Same until 8 sprints between CD and 8 between FA.

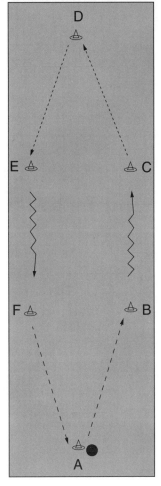

I do not understand why, but players usually thank me when it is all over. But a lot of them have also admitted that they occasionally swore at me under their breath. I can appreciate that. What they have to go through is no joke. We spend 4 or 5 days, or even longer, going to the limit. Always in just the right dosage, of course, because you must not push a player too far. It is important not to demand too much. After each drill, I ask the same question: "Feeling any pain?" because as soon as a player feels something, we stop, and the player goes back to physiotherapist Pim van Dord. Usually the player is too tired to do more than nod or shake his head. But that is all I need. I put a lot of faith in my own intuition. I am not the type of person who can spend lots of time considering how a player feels. I see how he feels. Not from his heart rhythm or other measurements, but simply from his face and his movements. Nor do I work with a stopwatch or anything like that. In this form of training in particular, you cannot afford to let yourself be distracted by tables and statistics. You have to take account of the specific characteristics, skills, strengths and weaknesses of the player concerned. I am more like a tailor who makes a made-to-measure suit than a salesman who prefers to take a ready-made suit from the rack. That is a good comparison. The players are put through training sessions that are completely tailored to their own personal circumstances, whereby the injury is of course a crucial starting point. It is therefore very important to have a good knowledge of a player before you start to work with him.

The satisfaction is great when a player succeeds in returning to the squad, not only for the player, but also for Bobby Haarms.

Not that they are fully fit again, because they have to get used to playing against resistance. But they are ready for it; they don't have to hold back. The only thing that I always say to them is that they should be careful, especially at the start of a training session. If I am still busy with them and the first players from the squad come onto the field, I always point out how badly most of them commence the session. What happens? They come out cold from the dressing room, carry 30 balls onto the field, and without carrying out any warming-up exercises they start shooting at goal as hard as they can. There are not many things that are worse for muscles or joints that have just recovered from an injury. Every player knows that it is not good for them, but soccer players are always so sure of themselves. I am 60 now and it is a long time since I played myself, but I remember that it was just the same in my day. You love playing, and you just cannot resist kicking a ball, especially at goal. But they will regret it if they kick the ground instead of the ball, and the muscle that has just been healed with so much pain and effort is torn or pulled. The ultimate objective is not that a player can rejoin the squad but that he can play competitively again. Only when that is achieved can I be satisfied. When I see them on the pitch, waving to the packed bleachers, with the bouquets of flowers in their hands, then I experience a silent moment of happiness."

Chapter 8
The Fitness and Coordination Specialists
Laszlo Jambor and Jos Geysel

Not many clubs employ a running coach, who forms part of the main coaching staff during first-team matches and therefore sits in the dugout. Ajax is one of the exceptions. This says a great deal about the significance that Louis van Gaal attaches to the work of Laszlo Jambor. Actually the term "running coach" does little justice to the contribution of the Hungarian physiologist and ex-basketball player. His know-how is not only used to supervise the running exercises of the first team and the youth teams at Ajax. For eight years Jambor has also been consulted daily on conditioning and strength training, and the recuperation of injured players.

After his career as a basketball player, Jambor became a famous coach in his native country of Hungary. He was the first coach of the famous Hungarian All Star team, which included a number of top Hungarian, American and Russian basketball players. He also taught at Hungary's largest sports academy, and this was of most importance for his work at Ajax. He taught technique, tactics and conditioning on the basis of physiological principles. Jambor himself says that this period was very significant.

In 1988, Jambor had his first contact with the coaching staff of Ajax, through Hungarian winger Paul Fischer who played for the Amsterdam club for a short time. At first a number of Ajax players questioned the value of Jambor's work. This was not surprising, because what they mainly wanted was to improve tactically and technically. However, they soon found that a better running technique and better physical coordination, as well as increased athleticism, also brought about improvements in their technical performance. From that time on, the turning and slalom movements and jumping exercises with sticks and gates have become as much a part of training sessions as positional games or finishing drills. Under Van Gaal, and at the express request of Youth Development Director Co Adriaanse, Jambor is also involved with the young players every day.

In Jambor's approach players of all ages always appear to be faster and more mobile than their opponents.

At Ajax, physical training is approached at three levels. All of the teams do physical coordination and speed training. Then, from the Under 16 teams upwards, soccer aerobics, muscle strengthening exercises and explosive strength training are added. Finally, even the youngest groups receive running training. The careful build up is especially clear in the video. Only the most obvious faults are corrected in these young players. And with the youngest children, only one aspect of running training is handled at any time.

Even Ajax's talented young players learn new movements rather awkwardly at first, because their muscles are too tense. However, the result of regular practice is that tension vanishes and the movements require less energy. Success is therefore brought about by constant repetition.

Coordination training

Why does the Ajax youth development program pay so much attention to footwork and the associated coordination training?

"The nervous system is such that the hands develop before the feet," says Laszlo Jambor. "This is why, when you start to work with young players, it is important not just to practice soccer drills but also to focus on the associated footwork. The nervous system is ready for this. It is a question of practicing coordination between the nervous system and footwork. Good footwork is crucial for any soccer player. You need to constantly adapt your manner of running to the situation. If there is plenty of room and the ball is a long way off, you will normally accelerate and take longer strides. In a small area, with the ball close by, you need to be sure that you can receive the ball at any moment, and also that you can change direction at any moment. You therefore need to take smaller steps without losing speed. Ajax frequently uses obstacles in training sessions devoted to this aspect. These force the players to adjust the length of their stride. The distance between the obstacles obviously depends on the age of the players and the coach's objectives. If a high frequency is required, the distance between the obstacles will be shorter. Higher obstacles can be used to help train the knee action. Obviously the height depends on the level of proficiency already achieved by the players. Higher obstacles should only be used when the players' technique is consistently good. All these exercises are used to promote the fine coordination between arms and legs.

Footwork is also the basis for a player's shooting technique. The Ajax philosophy is that its young players should carry out footwork exercises from the very beginning. This results in more "handy" movement during play. Actually it would be better to refer to it as more "footy" movement. This is why we train the youngsters in elements such as rate of stride, how to push off with their feet when they start to run, and the ability to turn quickly."

Speed training

What are the principles of speed training? First of all you have to understand why Ajax emphasizes starting and acceleration during training sessions. A soccer player runs in a very complex way during a game. You need to react constantly to the situation of play, and that involves continuous changes of speed and direction. The distance you cover lies between 8 and 13 kilometers. The distance you sprint in a game of soccer is between 3 and 20 yards, i.e. between 1 and 4 seconds. Occasionally you may need to sprint for longer, but sprinting at full speed for more than 5 seconds at a time is unusual.

Starting and acceleration capacity are a question of muscle power multiplied by the speed with which muscles contract. Scientific research has shown that acceleration is mostly determined by the pushing-off power of the first stride. This also uses up the most muscle power. The power that is injected into the push-off into the first stride is therefore very valuable. For purposes of training, it is necessary to differentiate between stationary, mobile and flying starts. My advice is not to carry out sprint training over the whole length of the sprint, but rather to practice an explosive start and, in particular, the first push-off.

In order to bring the available power to bear more quickly in the first stride, we often make the players carry out sprint starts on a slight slope. Immediately after this sprint start against less resistance, the start should be repeated on the pitch. This is how we at Ajax try to translate the higher movement frequency into a flat-surface situation. The faster first stride can also be practiced with an elastic rope, which gives a catapult effect to a player's speed off the mark.

Increasing the resistance will subsequently result in the sprint training having more effect. This is why we also work with weights during speed training. However, be warned, you should not start this before your technique is right. In addition, you need to select the resistance in such a way that your running technique remains good."

Sprints

According to Jambor there is one significant difference between a top team and a team in the sub-top: the quality of the sprints! "In general, top players not only start faster, but they also more frequently choose the right moment to start. In top games, there are numerous situations where you need to sprint. This is why we at Ajax put so much effort into improving starting technique and speed. However, Ajax's philosophy is that physical training and, by extension, speed training must always serve soccer purposes rather than being viewed as independent disciplines. You must never simply train for speed, but always ask yourself what sort of speed you will need, and in which situation. The way in which speed training is carried out at Ajax therefore results directly from an analysis of what is needed. All drills are derived from soccer situations.

Players are given less and less room to maneuver by their opponents. To gain a vital few yards of space they therefore have to put in more sudden sprints, or send their opponents the wrong way by feinting to go in one direction and then sprinting in another. The most important aspects are the moment of starting, the pulling away movement, and the disguised movement. These are all movements and actions without the ball, which result from communication between teammates. It is a question of reading and anticipating each other's movements. This requires a great deal of training in combined action. This is why so much attention is focused on small sided games and positional games at Ajax. However, even this approach sometimes involves training without the ball.

Your maximum speed off the mark with a ball at your feet is less than it is without a ball. The same applies to starting power. Your body becomes stronger and develops more physical power if it is challenged to go to the limit. In order to promote this development, you must ensure that the players regularly sprint and jump to their maximum during training sessions. In this way the limits of their performance are steadily pushed back. If training is carried out exclusively with the ball, the players cannot reach the limits of their maximum physical performance and cannot, therefore, extend these limits. The constant desire to push back the limits, the drive to improve, the desire to learn something new - these are attitudes that every Ajax soccer player must strive for, in both the short term and the long term."

Strength

According to Jambor, training to improve skills has nothing in common with training to increase sheer strength. "You need to be able to apply your strength. This involves dexterity and timing. This is what makes strength training for soccer so complex. It is so complex that it is best to incorporate physical strength exercises in a specific soccer situation or near-soccer situations. Some duels demand sudden, and others steady, muscle exertion. You have to train for duels in soccer situations. First with light resistance and then with more. In this way you can learn to brace your body in fractions of a second. The use of body muscles can be improved by exercising them separately. Soccer is not about how many kilometers you can run - after all, the ball is supposed to do the work. You often have to sprint to, from and with the ball. Repeating and sustaining the short sprints demanded in top soccer is what counts. And this is what training at Ajax is geared to: very fast footwork, short ground contact, fast rotation and runs, even when the players are extremely fatigued. The high intensity of training sessions is characteristic, particularly since Van Gaal has been with Ajax."

Tests

Even Jambor is not safe from the virus with which Van Gaal has infected everyone at Ajax: striving for ever greater perfection. However, he can benefit from the know-how of another physiologist brought in by Van Gaal: Jos Geysel. Since Geysel became involved, Jambor's drills have focused even more on the first stride, the first few yards, and running in all directions, including backwards.

In view of the constant pressure from the Ajax coaching staff to evaluate and adjust all sorts of aspects, it is almost a matter of course for the Ajax players to be regularly confronted with soccer tests. The Cooper test (how far can you run in twelve minutes?), which many soccer coaches use, especially when preparing for the season, is taboo at Ajax. It has too little relevance to soccer situations.

"I feel that every good soccer player should despise the Cooper test," says Jos Geysel. "Obviously it gives you an insight into your stamina, but it is far too unspecific in terms of soccer. The players have to run for far too long at the same speed.

At Ajax we prefer to use a number of shuttle-run tests:

In the shuttle-sprint test, the players sprint 5 x 10 yards in 3 series (see diagram). The first time they do not run flat out, then the best time achieved in the second and third runs is taken (the times are electronically measured). The shuttle-tempo test (see diagram) is run five minutes after the shuttle-sprint test. The players have to run the distances of 10, 20, 30, 40 and 50 yards at high speed. The aim is to run flat out for the entire 300 yards. Ten minutes later the players are given the shuttle-run test (see diagram). Each time they cover a distance of 20 yards, at a speed which is indicated by a signal on the sideline. You start at a speed of 8 km/h, and the tempo is continuously increased. Each player wears a heart-rate monitor during this test. In addition, the players are weighed prior to commencing the test, and their fat percentage is measured in the changing rooms. In just one and a half hours, this procedure provides you with a treasure trove of data concerning the physical condition of the entire squad. The tests provide an excellent insight into the players' condition. Condition is the sum of sprint, speed and stamina qualities in relation to the player's body. This involves much more than the stamina that can be measured with the Cooper test.

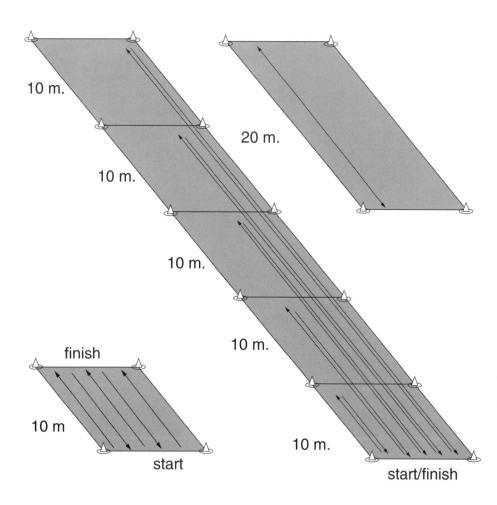

Do you know what was unusual? The first results of the shuttle-sprint tests at Ajax were disappointing! I had in my possession the results of the same tests by top field hockey players, and they turned out to be faster than the Ajax players on average. At that time everyone associated the name Ajax with fast and mobile players. Partly based on the results of scientific research by the Free University in Amsterdam, and following extensive discussions among the coaching staff, after the first test results were received a decision was made to incorporate more short interval work in the Ajax training sessions. After just one season, the Ajax players achieved better test results than the top field hockey players. This is highly motivating of course, but even more important is the fact that the new approach obviously gets results. The major credit for this has to go to a specialist like Jambor, who was immediately able to translate the change in philosophy into new, soccer-specific forms. No doubt Jambor's basketball background played a significant role in this. You can see that he knows just how important footwork is. Compare this with the athletics trainers who have been increasingly involved in training soccer players in recent years. I have my doubts when I hear them talk about high knee action, shoulders straight and still, an elegant running style and long strides. A soccer player who uses long strides will immediately fall prey to his opponent, because he will easily be deceived by a feint, or be knocked off balance. Contrary to other athletes, soccer players need to have a very high rhythm of movement. They constantly need to accelerate and decelerate quickly, run curves, weave and turn. These are the skills that have to be trained."

Science

"The new approach has borne fruit. The time is now ripe for the next step. At Ajax we are heavily involved in practical research in the field of sports science. For example, we are investigating the number of intervals - which work/rest ratios, and in which phase of the season - are optimal for the Ajax players. Currently this is still based far too much on intuition in the soccer world. Not that you will ever hear me say, forget intuition. As a coach you have to observe your players constantly, but you also have to communicate with them. Then you can automatically 'sense' when the time is right to prescribe some extra starting and sprinting practice. Van Gaal's experience indicates that, after a free day, players always take a little longer to focus both physically and mentally on the training. If you communicate with the players sufficiently, they will signal this themselves. In such a case, sprint training can have a psychological purpose. Another example demonstrates that sprint training need not only have a physiological purpose: Some months ago, two days after the Dutch international team had lost a game, Van Gaal had Jambor give the Ajax internationals an exhausting starting and sprinting training session. The next time, after a major win by the Dutch national team, he himself gave another drill to sharpen up Ajax's international players. Van Gaal decided on passing and kicking in a restricted space. But he demanded that this be carried out at the highest speed, and his coaching was aimed at making the players realize the importance of being sharp and alert, so they would recognize the right moment to play the ball. This was therefore starting, accelerating and sprint training using the ball.

Intuition remains extremely important, but I am also convinced that a scientific foundation can lead to more clearly defined decision making. Is the maximum duration of interval exertion for soccer players 30 or 45 seconds? How many repetitions are needed: 5, 10 or 20? How many series: 5, 8 or 10? What is the best ratio of work to rest: 1:1, 1:1.5 or 1.2? Each coach will admit to making these decisions mainly on the basis of his own intuition. Just as one coach will make his players do stomach muscle exercises 25 times, other colleagues consider 50 times too little. At Ajax the aim is to be able to make more informed decisions in this field, and to leave less to chance."

Young players

"Back to the tests. Ajax's young players are carrying out innovative work in this field. The highest youth teams also perform the shuttle-run tests. In addition they have to take a number of soccer-specific tests, designed by, among others, Co Adriaanse, which they take three times each year.

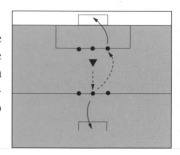

• Shooting technique (see diagram)
Two goals are placed 21 yards apart. Three balls are placed on the line marking the edge of the goal area and the line marking the edge of the penalty area. The balls must be struck directly into the empty goal, but not along the ground. The player is instructed which ball to play first, after which the sequence of the other balls is up to him. We are looking for cleverness and a preference for right or left. The test takes about 19 seconds of effort, and is always held by Ajax on synthetic grass when the weather is dry.

• Heading technique
The "header gallows" is used for this test. The player starts at a distance of 3 yards from the "gallows", and has to head the ball in such a way that it loops straight ahead and reaches at least the height of the point of attachment. The maximum height at which the ball can be suspended is measured. This test is used to measure both jumping power and heading skills.

• Sprinting and coordination capacity (see diagram)
A number of cones are deployed on the center circle and the center line. A player sprints to these cones and knocks them over. During this 17 second effort he has to stop suddenly several times, turn right and left, and demonstrate good footwork. This test can also be done with goals and balls.

• A specific sprint test
The young players sprint over a distance of 30 yards, and their times are measured at 5, 10, 15 and 20 yard intervals. This test shows the coordination coach, Jambor, the exact phase in which someone gains, or loses, most. He can draw his conclusions from this information for (individual) running training. Bobby Haarms closely adjusts his soccer-specific drills to the results of this test."

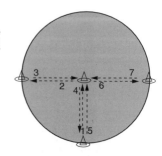

Chapter 9
The Ajax Youth Development Scheme with Co Adriaanse

Ajax and young soccer players. The two go together like the President and the White House. Every day Ajax receives requests from coaches all over the world, who want to take a look behind the scenes at the Ajax youth development program. The entire soccer world is aware of the fact that, year in, year out, Ajax has consistently produced a unique number of talented young players who have reached the absolute top.

The challenge that the Ajax youth development staff sets itself is to produce, every two seasons, three new youth players who can be integrated into the Ajax first team squad. The Ajax youth scheme was world famous even before Louis van Gaal came on the scene. The club's great successes were always based on players who had come through its own youth teams. World stars like Cruyff and Van Basten were surrounded by teammates with whom they had been together ever since they started to play.

The core of Van Gaal's Ajax is also made up of home-grown players who were given the opportunity to become stars by the Ajax coach. The De Boer twins, Edgar Davids, Clarence Seedorf, Patrick Kluivert, Michael Reiziger, all made their debut with Ajax at an age when players in other clubs are rarely given the chance. And seasoned players like Danny Blind and Frank Rijkaard are also products of the Ajax school.

Basically, Van Gaal continued the Ajax policy that paid dividends for many years. But Van Gaal would not be Van Gaal if he had failed to put his personal stamp on the Ajax system of youth development.

Very soon after his appointment, he saw it as his task to sharpen up the demands on the youth scheme, and to adjust them to the new developments at the top level of modern soccer. He made a sensible decision to help him achieve his target. Van Gaal kept his finger on the pulse of the youth development scheme while at the same time looking out for an assistant who could play an independent and creative part in meeting the new challenge.

His own work with talented Ajax players gave Van Gaal an accurate view of what needed to be improved. This made it easy for him to prepare a profile of the new "Director of Youth Development". In early 1992 one of the first candidates was Sef Vergoossen, a coach whose special vision of youth development has gained him an excellent reputation in the Netherlands. Unfortunately, at that time Vergoossen felt unable to give up the excitement of coaching in the premier division. Numerous other well known coaches applied to Ajax but, contrary to all expectations, Van Gaal selected a coach who had failed to serve out his contracts with two Dutch professional clubs - PEC Zwolle and FC Den Haag. In one case he left voluntarily, and in the other he was forced out.

This coach was Co Adriaanse, a man with a national reputation for a tough approach and a highly individual view of soccer. At first he was given a contract for one year only. Once more it became obvious that Van Gaal had taken a calculated risk. Well before the end of the first season, Adriaanse's contract was converted to one for an unlimited period. In the new Ajax structure, Van Gaal insisted that the Director of Youth Development should be on the same level as the Director of Professional Soccer, i.e. Van Gaal himself. There is no way in which a chief coach could have better emphasized that he considers youth development to be the very soul of the club. And, although he avoided interfering with the way Adriaanse ran the program, he insisted on daily reports concerning the developments in the youth development section. In addition, he spent so much time in Ajax's youth development complex that he was fully aware of the qualities of every young player, from the very youngest to the members of the reserve team.

"Continuity is particularly important in youth development." says Co Adriaanse, "This is why my position was created by the club's board, on the advice of Louis van Gaal. Until recently the Under 18 team coach regularly moved on to the first team, leaving a gap in the youth development scheme. This is what happened when coaches such as De Mos, Beenhakker and Van Gaal moved on, but this is now a thing of the past. As Director of Youth Development, I now have to concentrate on long-term planning.

In April 1992 I did not have to think very long about the offer from Ajax. Involvement with Ajax's lifeline to the future is an additional challenge for me as an Amsterdammer, and I was convinced that I already fitted Ajax's job description. It was also a long-term career move, something I had long been looking for. I have always felt that the biggest drawback for a coach is the burning question at the end of each season: Can I stay? This does not suit my character. I want to be able to make the decisions relevant to my life and career myself. If you work as a chief coach for a marginal team, you are constantly embarking on mission impossible."

Communications

After his appointment, Adriaanse put his stamp, step by step, on every facet of the Ajax youth development program.

"I started with internal communications. A large number of club officials are involved in the Ajax youth development program, and it is a considerable task to ensure that everyone is well informed and that everyone is pulling in the same direction."

Adriaanse points at the huge planning sheet behind his desk and continues: "We have fixed consultations every week. For example, I talk to the co-directors at Ajax at agreed times, i.e. to Louis van Gaal as the Director of Professional Soccer, and the Commercial and Financial Directors. Set hours are also planned for individual discussions with the youth coaches and the match secretaries.

I also place great value on the opinions of our chief scout, Ton Pronk. He is a sort of red line, running right through the club. Pronk handles all the scouting work, is always available to deputize for other coaches, and his contribution to the selection procedure is extremely valuable.

This procedure takes account of numerous opinions, set out in reports. The coach, Pronk and I all have a vote, and we also consider the recommendations from the team captain. In principle, an Ajax youth player is only a member for one year. An average of 30 of the 160 youth players drop out after one season. In this context, Ajax has to implement a tough selection procedure.

Communication with parents is also important. A youngster who plays for Ajax is often already a mini-star in his own environment, even though, in Ajax terms, he still has a lot to learn. This means that parents must be kept well informed of what is happening, because otherwise the youngster may find himself listening to two different versions of the same story every day. It goes without saying that he will always lean towards the more favorable version, and this is usually bad for his development as a soccer player.

One of the first visible products that Adriaanse developed during his first year was a comprehensive report on each of Ajax's young hopefuls. Twice a year, in April and December, the report is discussed with both the player and his parents. The subjects usually found on a school report have been replaced by the following soccer elements, which are subdivided into a number of categories:

• ball control, dribbling, passing, beating an opponent, shooting, speed of action, attacking headers, scoring ability, crosses, speed on the ball;

• 1 to 1 duels, defending, defensive headers, sliding tackles, tackling, attacking the ball;

• combination skills, overview, positional play, adherence to assigned tasks;

• athletic personality, speed off the mark, speed from 0 to 10, from 10 to 30, and above 30 yards, mobility, strength in the tackle, stamina, running skills and jumping power;

• charisma, leadership ability, match mentality, attitude towards others, teammates, coach, referee, etc., receptivity to coaching, and ability to withstand pressure;

• other information: modest, cheeky, creative, plays in the service of others, character player, technical player, right footed, left footed, two footed.

Twice a year the players' coaches rate them on a scale of 1 to 9 for each element. We have not deliberately left out the rating "10", it simply cannot be easily accommodated by our software."

Analysis

The second step that Co Adriaanse took at Ajax was to prepare a strengths and weaknesses analysis.

"At Ajax a lot is done on the basis of intuition. This has led to a typical Ajax culture, with a high yield in terms of the numbers of young soccer players who succeed in making the grade. In recent years no less than seventy players from the Ajax school have turned professional in the Netherlands or abroad, and a number of them have become millionaires. We intend to maintain this culture in the future, but if we are to remain ahead of our financially powerful competitors, we have to move forward. We should be able to manage this by giving even more thought and attention to our strengths and, more important still, our weaknesses. Our target is to prepare two or three talented players for the top every two seasons, taking account of the various positions in the team. If you can maintain this policy for ten years, you are in clover.

In our thorough analysis, we soon found more strengths than weaknesses. We use the acronym TIPS to describe the strong points of a young Ajax player, and this term soon became familiar in the Dutch soccer world.

The T stands for technique. An Ajax junior must be in control of the ball.

The I stands for intelligence and insight. The ability to observe and think ahead, so that you can come up with specific plays that your opponent will not expect.

The P stands for personality. An Ajax talent must be able to communicate well with others, provide leadership, be creative, show flair and daring, be receptive to his fellow players, and be able to work in a disciplined manner.

The S stands for speed, which is essential for every Ajax player. Speed off the mark, mobility and speed over longer distances. The Ajax scouts are always on the lookout for I, P and S, because these are very difficult to influence. Technique can always be improved. The selection criteria used by the scouts means that Ajax's juniors are technically gifted, soccer wise, interesting personalities, with good basic speed.

If you take a critical look at the shortcomings of the average Ajax youngster, you will see that he often lacks the mental and physical stamina needed at the very top. The fighting spirit is sometimes lacking, and the young Ajax players often feel superior to their opponents, for whom the games against Ajax are always the highlight of the year, at all levels.

The Ajax youth players are often inclined to look down on their opponents. Naturally this "Amsterdam bluff" has its advantages, but it does mean that you tend to be insufficiently critical of your own play. In addition, most Ajax defenders are too small by international soccer standards, and this becomes obvious during competitions against top foreign clubs.

Naturally we have considered all sorts of methods of combating these shortcomings. The coaches will have to be more critical and take a tougher line with their charges. You could specifically select a number of players for each team, whose task would be to keep the other players sharp and alert during training and matches. In training you could use more drills that emphasize aspects such as gaining possession of the ball, physical strength, and switching over quickly when possession is lost. We, as Ajax, will also have to participate in more international competitions, including those for older age categories. Perhaps we need to take a look at what we can learn from other types of sport in this context. Some martial arts could possibly contribute an element of added value. We also confront the Ajax juniors with aerobics. The exercises are good for coordination, which is extremely important, and they promote efficient movement and suppleness, as well as helping to train 'forgotten' muscle groups. Aerobics also introduces variety, and the choice of music allows you to lay a link to the world of your talented young players. I only hope that after reading of these benefits, youth trainers at amateur clubs will not make a beeline for aerobics. If you only have a few hours available for soccer coaching, then obviously you should focus exclusively on soccer drills. At Ajax, half an hour of aerobics is an extra.

In any case, I quickly came to the conclusion that the structure of the Ajax training program needed to be changed if the physical and mental toughness of the club's young players was to be improved.

At the end of my first year as the Director of Youth Development I formulated my ideas as follows: Now, and in future, an Ajax junior must be selected on the basis of ball skills, creativity, speed, soccer insight and personality. Youngsters who exhibit these properties often lack the required mental toughness, physical strength or the ideal character. They need to learn to deal with disappointment. Players with less natural talent have to fall back on their strength and fighting spirit to compensate for a lack of cleverness and technique. It is essential to take account of these facets during training, but not at the scouting stage. This basic principle sets Ajax apart from many other professional clubs, both in the Netherlands and abroad."

Points of departure

After carrying out this analysis of strengths and weaknesses, Co Adriaanse started to prepare his development plan.

"Naturally Ajax's playing philosophy existed before I came here. Ajax players must provide entertainment. You are an artist, and you have to compete with other forms of entertainment. And you always try to win. This can be done by playing on the opposition's half of the field, by creating lots of goal-scoring chances, by using fore-checking when you lose possession. You also have to be able to operate within a 3:4:3 concept. These are the familiar points of departure for Ajax's style of play.

In order to be able to achieve these objectives, you need to find multi-functional players. They have to be able to switch positions on the wings and in the central backbone of the team. A left winger needs to be able to play at left back or as a left midfielder. By the year 2000 there will be no room at the top for players who are restricted to a single position. I am sure of this, and obviously we take it into account in our scouting activities.

Every Ajax youth eleven has 16 players. There are two goalkeepers. Four right footed players are selected for positions 2, 6 and 7, four left footed players for positions 5, 8 and 11, three players for 3 and 4, and finally three players for 9 and 10. This applies from the Under 10 team up to the first eleven. During the players' development, therefore, they play in the two or three positions within the team for which they have been selected."

Systems

What is new is Adriaanse's idea that Ajax's young hopefuls must learn about more than just the 4:3:3 concept during their soccer development.

"From the Under 16 team onward, we want our players to master more than one system (4:4:2 and 4:3:2:1). We consider this important, because it means that the players are confronted with new spatial relationships with regard to their teammates and opponents, and have to search for new solutions."

Discipline

Adriaanse emphasizes discipline in the same way as Van Gaal, from the very start of a player's development at Ajax.

"In addition to the playing philosophy, I am also concerned with questions of discipline. Society is changing in many ways. The individual is becoming more important, standards are blurring, and for a long time 'achievement' was almost a dirty word. This was reflected in sports education, where pleasure was suddenly more important than achievement. In our society, many people do not know their neighbors, let alone what they do for a living.

However, the laws of top level sport are unchanging and, in a team, you are dependent on your neighbor. This is why behavior in the group is extremely significant for an Ajax youngster, and that means he has to learn consideration for others. If you cannot do this off the pitch, you will have problems on the pitch. This is why, in my first year, I gave the coaches a number of disciplinary rules, which all players must adhere to absolutely. Agreements have been reached with regard to behavior during games and practice. Players are expected to be punctual, to remove their caps when they enter the canteen or locker rooms, may not wear earrings, and shin guards are compulsory. Discipline must not be absolutely rigid, but it is essential that the same rules apply at all levels. If a player commits a serious foul, and the referee fails to see it, it should never be possible for one coach to simply overlook the foul if another would react by removing the player from the pitch. Nor should it be possible for the rules of behavior at mealtimes to differ from one team to another. This is the reason why I have put the regulations down in writing."

Development plan

In his second season, Adriaanse started to formulate the technical details of his development plan.

"This was a pretty big job, since, obviously, the principles have to be discussed with the entire coaching staff. Naturally we started at the beginning by formulating the requirements for the 8 to 12 age group. Then we looked at the 12 to 14, the 14 to 16, and the 16 to 20 age groups."

Adriaanse gives an example of the demands Ajax makes on a 12 year-old youngster. What must he be competent in when he has completed the first phase of his development at Ajax?

"We look at eight different areas: technique, tactics, know-how, running and strength training, personality forming, coaching situations, training and matches. Technique is most important for the 8 to 12 age group. What is in the description? They have to learn to control the ball with every part of both feet and in all directions. This sentence says it all. The Ajax youth coach must be sufficiently creative to incorporate this principle in his training sessions. I do not prepare full training schedules, because this would restrict the way a coach operates. I may well write down some important drills, but otherwise the youth coaches must be competent enough to invent drills to help them achieve their objectives. For example, we frequently use Coerver drills. All the coaches have the Coerver video film which shows these techniques, and can make their selection from it. I do not prescribe this, but I do, of course, assess the end product: are the 12 year-olds as technically skilled as we would like?

Other technical demands in the first phase include:
combining ball control and speed in complicated situations where there is an element of resistance;
- ability to use both feet to side-foot and semi-side-foot the ball and kick it with the instep, both along the ground and through the air, over short distances;
- taking and cushioning the ball with all parts of the body;
- juggling the ball with every part of the body except the arms;
- passing accurately from a standing position and while on the move;
- accurate shooting at goal;
- working on varied crosses;
- learning the basic heading technique, without resistance;
- developing and stimulating body swerves and feints
- learning techniques for taking the ball past an opponent;
- learning to shield the ball;
- the throw in;
- learning to take a penalty.

As far as tactics are concerned the following principles apply to the youngest group:
- running into space to receive the ball;
- positions in the length and breadth of the field;
- linking up, linking back;
- taking up position to receive the ball;
- playing from your own position;
- taking over the position of another player;
- learning to play in another position;
- looking beyond the ball;
- deciding the moment of choice between passing and making an individual run;
- learning to shield the ball when dribbling and passing;
- covering on the inside;
- covering the most dangerous opponent.

These are the objectives that the players must have achieved by the time they move up to the 12-14 age group.

It goes without saying that the coach takes account of the age and level of skill of the players in relation to the application of these principles.

In the field of soccer know-how the first targets are:
- learning the rules of the game;
- learning to keep their boots in good condition;
- learning to recognize the Ajax system of play ;
- learning to look after their bodies;
- acquiring knowledge of diet in the context of matches and training;
- learning knowledge of the rules of soccer and Ajax's own specific culture.

Running and strength training involves:
- learning the principles of a good running technique;
- coordinated running;
- learning to jump by taking off from one leg and from two legs;
- maintaining and improving suppleness;
- learning to use the body during duels;
- strength training by making use of the player's own body weight;
- learning to avoid an opponent, sliding tackle or tackle;
- sprinting in all directions;
- learning to use a shoulder charge.

Ajax's running coach, Laszlo Jambor, gives weekly training sessions to teach the 8 to 12 year-olds how to run well and functionally.

When it comes to personality forming, Ajax makes high demands even on the youngest players:
- learning a sporting attitude, in which respect for the opponent is central;
- learning to communicate with teammates, coaches and team support staff;
- learning to be open to the opinions of others;
- accepting leadership;
- learning to accept the referee's decisions;
- learning to be critical of their own achievements;
- learning to analyze their own game;
- learning to conform to the Ajax rules;
- learning to listen to the coach;
- learning that soccer is a team sport;
- experiencing the rudiments of team building;
- learning to concentrate;
- learning to be responsible for equipment;
- learning to avoid injury;
- learning to listen to their bodies.

In practice

Although it is essential to formulate objectives, paper is still just paper. How do things work in practice? Ajax considers that the ability to recognize talent in a seven year-old, and forecast how it will develop, is as difficult as it is important. Potential height can be defined at an early stage from x-rays of the hand bones. Height is important for keepers and defenders.

The first year 8 to 10 age group is the most important in terms of scouting. Basically a new team, preferably with 16 players, must be ready each year. However, Ajax scouts exclusively on the basis of quality. This season only 14 7 year-olds matched the criteria, even though the Ajax scouts observed thousands of 8 to 10 year-olds during the so-called talent days on location (TOL) at youth soccer clubs in the region and during the weekly matches played by youth soccer clubs.

Even for the expert Ajax scouts, recognizing genuine talent at such an early age is a difficult task. Some of the children may have joined the club just recently. Is it right to give them preference over others of the same age with more soccer experience?

Even in the 8 to 10 age group, Ajax takes note of how well a talented youngster runs. During the two week test period, when a potential new 8 to 10 year-old is assessed on the basis of six activities, coordination coach Jambor is asked for an opinion.

Another problem involved in selecting 8 to 10 year-olds is the difference in mental development encountered in this age group. Some are still almost infants and are impossible to motivate, because of the shortness of their attention span. A child like this is rejected. If you join Ajax, you have to be coachable and able to understand instructions, even if you are only 7. The child's environment is also considered during the first phase. What sort of support is provided by the parents? How is the child dressed?, How does he behave? Is he punctual? If adequate attention is paid to the initial selection, there will be no need to make too many subsequent adjustments further up the age range - this is the Ajax philosophy.

When a 7 year-old has passed this strict selection procedure and is allowed to wear his Ajax shirt at last, his first period with the Amsterdam club will be devoted to learning the basic skills. He first needs to master various techniques if he is later to be able to make the right choices in the various positions within the Ajax system. For this reason the drills developed by Wiel Coerver are used extensively for the 8 to 10 and 10 to 12 age groups. According to the coaching staff, these drills help children not only to use their feet more skillfully, but also to improve their balance, speed up their rhythm, pull away to the right and left, and use every part of their feet.

But it is typical for the 8 to 10 age group that each child plays for himself rather than combining with the others. In addition, the children move towards the ball and not away from it, and are inclined to play the ball forward and not to the side or backwards. These characteristics are in complete contrast to the Ajax vision.

Technique

Ajax uses all kinds of balls to improve the technique of its talented beginners. This is just a translation of street soccer into the practical reality of the 8 to 10 year old youngsters of today. Children used to use all sorts of balls, hard balls, leaking but heavy balls, tennis balls, when they kicked around on the streets. In this way they acquired an excellent "feel" for the ball and, in playing, learned how to use their feet better.

The 8 to 10 and 10 to 12 year old players train regularly with tennis balls, small leather Umbro balls or foam rubber balls. The theory is that children who learn to control such a small ball will subsequently find it easier to control a normal sized ball. A foam rubber ball has to be treated really gently otherwise it will fly away, and a tennis ball requires a lot of coordination and concentration.

Each 8 to 10 year old player who starts at Ajax is also given a ball in a net, the so-called "soccer pal." He has to work with this until December. Once each week the coach of the 8 to 10 players goes through a series of drills with the soccer pal, and the players have to do homework with it in their own time. After the winter break the E players should have learned so much that they can work on their ball control at home without the net.

Tactics

The youngest Ajax players are also coached in tactics. The Under 10 team plays games of 11 v 11 in the Under 12 competition, i.e. against players who are 2 years older. And once every two weeks the 8 to 10 age group coach plays an additional friendly game against a youth soccer club which, after a written request, receives an invitation to play against Ajax. In addition the 8 to 10 year-olds learn the rudiments of the Ajax system in a fun way.

For example, the Ajax system is based on always trying to play on the opposition's half of the pitch. This means that space is restricted, and each player has to create his own space. The player in possession of the ball must always look for opportunities to pass backwards if a forward pass is impossible. The youngest players learn this tactical principle in a fun way from the start. The 8 to 10 year-olds are given the following problem to solve: "I came to a house and I wanted to go in through the front door. That was not possible. It was locked and nobody wanted to open it. Yet I still got inside. How did I do that? Most of the youngsters want to solve the problem by breaking open a window. "No", says the coach, "I went round to the side and found the side door open. But last time I went there, the side door was locked too. How did I get in that time?" Most of the youngsters know the answer by now. "Through the back door". Subsequently the link to the Ajax system is made. The result is that Ajax's under 10 players can be heard to say: "If we can't play forward, we will have to try the flanks, and if that is not possible, we will have to play backwards, but a defender will have to be in position so that we can play the ball back."

Coaches

"Obviously the ability to explain things in terms that young children can understand is a gift. This is why Ajax has made a conscious decision to use a young coach with teaching abilities to coach the youngest players. He has to be young because the age gap should never be too wide. The coaches of the Under 10 and Under 12 teams must be able to comprehend the world of their charges, their use of language and their way of contributing to the matter in hand. Only then can he create drills that will slot into the world of a 7 to 10 year-old, while fulfilling the targets of the Ajax youth development philosophy. These coaches need to be mentally and physically in peak condition. And they must be able to set the perfect example. For example, the Ajax philosophy says that much more can be achieved with the Wiel Coerver drills by demonstrating what you mean than by explaining everything in detail - a good example can achieve more than a thousand words.

Putting together a team of coaches with this level of expertise is an important task for me as the Director of Youth Development. A basic principle is that every youth coach at Ajax must be happy with his position within the team. He must not think in terms such as, "I am now the Under 12 team coach, but I would rather be coaching the 14 to 16 year-olds, because this makes a better impression on outsiders." Within Ajax, there is no room for anyone who wants to elbow his way to the top. Every coach is expected to be happy with his position and to realize that his task is a very important one. As far as the Ajax board is concerned, the coach for the 8 to 10 year-olds is just as important as the coach for the 16 to

18 year-olds. The coach of the Under 18 team needs to be able to tell a good story, be convincing, capable of analyzing a match. He must be able to explain in accurate terms why a player keeps repeating the same mistake. He also needs to be able to think of drills to help correct the mistake. This demands a different set of skills to those of the coach of the under 10 players. This is why, in the Ajax philosophy, it is unthinkable that an Under 10 team coach should have the ambition to coach the Under 18 team in a few years time, or that an older coach should feel he could "take it easy" by coaching the 8 to 10 year-olds. Together the youth coaches form a team, although each must remain ambitious in his own way. The same applies to all the different Ajax team units, board, medical staff, coaching staff, team captains, scouting team.

Every youth coach has a limited amount of freedom of action within the Ajax system. First of all he must always think of the whole picture. The point of departure is the match, and the basis is the Ajax system of play, which runs like a thread through the entire club. This is one of the major differences compared with other clubs. Other professional soccer clubs tend to think in compartments. The compartments are put together in the hope of forming a complete structure, i.e. the first team. Before they start, the builders have no idea what the finished structure will look like.

At Ajax the youth coaches and players know from the word go exactly how the finished structure should look: the desired system of play is totally familiar. Coaches and players think in terms of this system of play at all times. The coaches must always create drills which are related to the system of play and the associated positions.

Other requirements have also been formulated for the coaches. Every training session must have an objective, and although it must be hard work it must also be enjoyable for the players. In addition the youth coaches must be skilled in situational coaching. This in turn demands a considerable talent for improvisation, if they are to be able to react immediately to the various situations that can arise during a training session. The Ajax philosophy is as follows: You can learn a brilliant book full of coaching drills by heart, but the ability to act at the right moment, to make an accurate analysis and to show how things should be done, is much more important. That is the heart of the matter! And it is just as important that every player, from the youngest to the first eleven, realizes and accepts that the coach knows best. A coach can soon lose his credibility if he stops play at the wrong moment, or talks rubbish. The same applies if too little instruction is given. Only by choosing the right moment, and making constructive statements, can players be improved. This is the subject of a great deal of discussion between members of the coaching staff at Ajax. Anyone lacking these youth coaching characteristics will never make it at Ajax. Ajax's young players have to be sharp at all times, both mentally and physically, This can only be the case if the Ajax coaches are too.

Every week I meet with each youth coach at a regular time. I watch each team play at least once every two weeks. The meetings are usually concerned with discussions about the individual players. For example, I will consult with a youth coach if he feels that a certain player should no longer be playing in a specific position. The team may be stronger if he is left at that position, but the player's future within the Ajax system may well be in other positions, and this is what counts. In such a case, at Ajax the interests of the team must always be subjugated to the interests of the individual player.

Twice each year, all the players are assessed on forty elements. These assessments result in one of three recommendations:

A - stay
B - doubtful (B/A doubtful/stay)
C - go (B/C doubtful/go)

I make this decision which is then communicated to the youth player (in the case of the 8 to 10, 10 to 12 and 12 to 14 age groups, the parents are present at the meeting)."

Survival of the fittest

"Once the Ajax pupils have reached the age of 12, they enter the second stage of training in the 12 to 14 age group.

This is the age at which many of the youngsters are faced with accelerated physical growth. In this phase it is not unusual for the coaching staff to make mistakes. Boys who seem to be too small, but do show good potential, are often rejected on the grounds that they are physically incapable of competing with their own age group at this moment in time. The other side of the coin is that, due to their fast increase in height, youngsters who mature earlier often look as though they are unable to play soccer any more. For this reason, Ajax proposes to start up research into the delaying influence of the growth spurt on the soccer development of the 12 to 14 age group.

This is also a significant age group, because actual matches play a larger role. Boys of 13 and 14 already have more strength and speed, and are able to move the ball over long distances. This latter is a crucial factor in the Ajax system. Youngsters in the 12 to 14 age group have already undergone four years of Ajax training. In an enjoyable way they have already learned a great deal about making choices during a game.

The most stringent selection criteria are applied to the players in the second year of the Under 14 level. Young players who leave Ajax still head the scouting lists of other clubs, and are much sought after. Ajax does not exclude the possibility of their return at a later date."

Informatics

"Although a large number of Ajax's young players make the breakthrough, many fall by the wayside at the final step. I do not accept this as a matter of course. I sift through all the details, looking for causes, and consider what conclusions I should draw, in terms of making changes to scouting and internal selection.

If this is your objective and you require more assurance at the moment when you make your final judgment about the selections for the new season, you need a great deal of data. Observations by the coaches, and the intuitive feeling that this player will fit the Ajax pattern, and that one will not, remain the most important criteria, but you must be able to support intuition with facts. This is why I opted to store all the details of the young players in the computer. Together with a programmer I have developed a comprehensive computer program. Every week a clerk enters the relevant data. The program makes a number of fields available for the 160 youth players. After every match I receive an Ajax match form for each player. This contains coded basic information (position, goal, assist, red or yellow card), his role in the match (in the starting line-up or substitute, substituted, brought on, dropped out through injury, suspended, did not play due to injury, sick) and an assessment (bad, average, satisfactory, good, very good). These data are entered each week. With regard to the positions, the monitor shows a soccer field, so that I can see at a glance what positions a player was used in.

The medical records and school records of each player are also stored in the computer. It is well known that we at Ajax give education a high priority. When we go abroad we regularly take along a study coordinator, who has examination exercises with him in sealed envelopes. We have rejected the idea of putting all our talented youngsters into the same school. It is essential for the development of a child's personality that he should be allowed to grow up in his own environment. This means in his own family, in his own street, with his own friends, and at a school of his own choice. Keeping soccer players together all day long soon leads to the emergence of a group mentality, which you have to conform to in order to survive. This is always detrimental to the development of the individual personality, and it is why Ajax has never favored the idea of boarding school. We do have a system of guest families, but these are selected for their similarity to the actual family of the foreign youngster.

The choice of good educational support demands a great deal of ingenuity, thought and time, in terms of timetable planning, arrangements and transport. But this is an absolute necessity. Fortunately we have experts of long standing in the fields of educational support here at Ajax.

Our computer program allows us to combine this mountain of data to suit our own ends, and after a number of years we should have enough information to show why some of the talented youngsters did or did not make the grade. However, it is essential never to apply these conclusions to each individual youngster. What will probably become clear is which elements of scouting, selection procedure and development need extra attention. For example, the data could well indicate the best time to promote a certain type of player to a higher age group category, or which type of player will have only a small chance of success with Ajax. In this way, it is likely that an Ajax standard will emerge."

The future

"I always want to be able to do new things. This is essential for a Director of Youth Development at a club like Ajax. If the time comes when I realize that my function has become reduced to monitoring and maintenance, I will leave.

At the end of my fourth season with Ajax, hopefully, I need not fear that there will be a lack of demand for my powers of creativity and innovative capacity. The familiar De Meer stadium closed its doors to the youth players, too, in the summer of 1996. A major move was on the cards. I rejected a generous offer of the position of coach to a German Bundesliga club in anticipation of a new challenge awaiting at Ajax.

Looked at objectively, the move to new premises is a logical step. The De Meer stadium has long been unable to satisfy the logistical wishes and demands of a top club. This also applies to the accommodation for the youth players. A small club house, some very modest locker rooms, a single playing field, a small synthetic grass pitch, and a container converted to provide an office for the Director.

One of the major advantages of "Voorland" was that, in De Meer, the first team's accommodation and that of the young players was separated only by a wooden bridge. On the one hand, this was a symbolic obstacle, which the talented young players had to surmount as a first step towards joining the first eleven. At the same time, the bridge acted as a continuous link between the young players and the rest of Ajax. This ensured that coaches, (ex) players, supporters and board members were regularly to be seen in the "home" of the Ajax youngsters. And the young players felt an actual and imaginary link to their idols in the first team. For many years this was the secret of the indefinable but ever present feeling that "Ajax is one big family".

Unity

"In the new environment, which was given the highly appropriate name 'The Future', the physical distance between the first team and the youngsters has grown.

For this reason, I consider it an important task to ensure that there is sufficient contact between the young players and the first team. Fortunately the ArenA, the new home ground of Ajax, is visible from 'The Future'. In addition, the futuristic lines of the ArenA, with all their semi-circular shapes, have consciously been incorporated in the exterior of 'The Future'. In this way uniformity has been maintained.

The result is amazing. Anyone who remembers the old youth accommodation, which would have caused many an amateur club embarrassment, will be unable to believe his eyes on first sight of 'The Future'. Fantastic bleachers and three grass playing fields, which can handle at least four hundred playing hours each year without any loss of quality. Three training fields, a gigantic club house with expensive wood block floors, a gymnasium, a swimming pool where injured young players can practice aqua-jogging, a medical room with the latest equipment, and much more. Nowadays an average professional club would have every right to go green with envy at the sight of the Ajax youth accommodation. The sight of all this luxury makes it difficult to believe this is a club where economies were made on Christmas card stamps just prior to the start of the Van Gaal era.

Although we might appear to have a perfect coaching environment we can never be satisfied. Despite the immense amount of work involved in moving, I still had to reserve a large number of hours for improving the content of the Ajax youth development scheme.

To compensate for the loss of street soccer in the busy city of Amsterdam, we have developed a soccer playground for the youngest Ajax players. Twice a week the 8 to 12 year-olds can enjoy themselves there, playing soccer tennis, header volley ball, keeping the ball in the air, or small sided games. The soccer playground underlines the Ajax philosophy that young players cannot spend too much time with the ball.

The way each young player runs is recorded on video. Impressions are made of each youngster's feet for the early prevention of back injuries.

Every Ajax youngster now has his own log book, in which he can record all the information he receives during the years of his Ajax education. And - a recent innovation - he also has a "passport", in which his requirements for each year are exactly recorded."

Daily organization

"The daily organization has also been perfected even further. As always the motto is attention to every detail. The oldest youth players need more coaching during training sessions than the very youngest. This is why the training ground for the oldest of the young players is located furthest away from the adjacent freeway.

Preparing a training schedule is no mean feat at Ajax. Educational support (a priority item at Ajax), transportation, meals, etc. must all be taken constantly into consideration. In addition, many Ajax youngsters are given both aerobic and running training in addition to the normal soccer training sessions. The separate training for goalkeepers also has to be fitted into the schedule.

At the same time, the full-time youth coaches at Ajax coach a number of teams. This is another factor that has to be considered. Daily organization is a real puzzle, especially when you remember that enough space must be left for discussions, etc. We must never be satisfied, and continue to keep a critical eye on each other.

The constant will to improve. This is the principle of Ajax and the Ajax youth development scheme."

Chapter 10
The High Point:
The Victory over AC Milan

Ask any top sportsman to name his ultimate objective and the answer will be: to become the world champion or to win a gold medal at the Olympic Games. In December 1995 the Ajax players achieved this objective by beating the Brazilian team, Grémio, in a game that went to a penalty shoot-out. For the umpteenth time in a unique year, Amsterdam prepared to honor its idols.

The World Club Championship was the crowning glory of a year of superlatives. Of 52 official games at national and international level, Ajax won 43 and suffered only one defeat, in March, in a Dutch cup tie against arch rival Feyenoord Rotterdam. The team scored 155 goals and conceded only 29.

Theoretically, the victory against Grémio was the high point, but in Europe, winning the Champions League fired the popular imagination more. The fact that such an old established institution as the Italian club AC Milan was defeated in the final certainly had a lot to do with this. The win, the high point of the Van Gaal era, was achieved on May 24, 1995, in the Ernst Happel stadium in Vienna. The following is a reconstruction of the preparations and the final itself.

Preparations

The preparations for the final of the Champions League began in mid May. It is just two days since Louis van Gaal held up the Dutch Championship shield before a hundred thousand fanatical supporters in the center of Amsterdam. Before the first training session, to the amazement of a number of diehard Ajax supporters, Van Gaal congratulates them on their club! In the dressing room he tells the players to forget all about their recent triumph; today they must start to prepare themselves for the all-important European Cup clash with AC Milan, just 9 days away. Vienna awaits.

The training session is held on the main pitch. A typical Ajax training session, starting with lots of short interval work under the guidance of running coach Jambor. The players exude athleticism. Later they are asked to demonstrate their shooting skills with the ball. It's immediately obvious that at this level it's more a question of practicing their skills rather than improving them, since a high degree of perfection has already been attained. Van Gaal, however, is quick to point out that even the most experienced players can always pick up new skills. The second part of the training session clearly shows how Ajax will confront AC

Milan. Louis van Gaal's intuitive creativity has come up with an 8 against 8 positional game in a strip of the pitch adjacent to the halfway line. When one team wins possession, one of its players must immediately sprint into the other half to receive a long pass under pressure. Other players then have to support the attack as quickly as possible. The message to his players was clear: in the European Championship final, Ajax will have to play more in their own half than usual. They will have to exploit the space that this creates in AC Milan's half of the field. The intention was clear, but even Ajax players sometimes allow their minds to wander. Van Gaal won't stand for this. As the training session progresses his annoyance increases and his voice grows louder.

Drills

After the training session, Van Gaal agrees that he was not satisfied: "I fully understand the players. They've been celebrating for the last two days. On Sunday I went along with them, and yesterday I left them to go out on the town by themselves. It's not exactly surprising that they lack sharpness during the first training session. As the coach, however, I have to ensure that they get back into the swing of things as soon as possible. It wasn't just any old training session. The moves we practiced took account of AC Milan's style of play.

AC Milan is one of the only teams in Italy that plays to win, and not just to avoid defeat. This means they come at their opponents. We want to help them in this by defending more in our own half than usual, so that we can take advantage of the extra space this creates in their half. I'd like to try this out in the game against Feyenoord a few days before the final, but during the first training session the 8 against 8 positional game was already based on this tactic. Naturally I've spoken to the players about this. I then expect them to get down to it and put the events of the last few days behind them. Initially this was certainly not the case. Neither side played as a unit, whether it was in possession or pressing, nor did the players pay sufficient attention to the size of the area where the positional play took place. It's my job to intervene and get them moving alertly again."

Of the team's next opponents, Van Gaal says clearly: "Whatever the outcome, AC Milan is my preferred choice of opponent in the final. I'd much rather play against a team like AC Milan than against Parma or Paris St. Germain.

AC Milan plays, just as Ajax, to win. The two other European teams I mentioned are primarily interested in avoiding defeat. They hang back, waiting for their opponents to come at them, and then use the space this creates in their opponents' half. Both teams have the players for that type of game: Ginola and Asprilla in particular.

A team like AC Milan, on the other hand, which likes to play in the opposition's half of the field, suits us better in principle. If AC Milan decides to hold back, then that's not really a problem either. After all, we're used to playing in our opponents' half. That's when Ajax is at its strongest, because we manage to keep every position covered. The only problem will be that I will probably need a lasso to hold my players back. They tend to become over enthusiastic". After making this analysis on the eve of the final in the Ernst Happel stadium, Van Gaal quickly adds, "If I knew for certain that AC Milan would leave the initiative to us, I would obviously have chosen a different approach to training today. For example, playing the ball to the advanced striker and explaining when and how other players can come up in support against a team like AC Milan.

I regard the creative use of coaching drills as a daily challenge. Carrying out the right drill at the right moment. Then you watch to see that the drill is carried out properly. You coach, and if something happens that you didn't intend, you have to correct it immediately. That's how coaching sessions should be carried out."

Detail

Only brand new Adidas Questra balls were used during the training session. Van Gaal smiles when we remark on this: "Today is the first time we've played with that ball. It's the one that will be used in the final against AC Milan. It's a completely different type of ball to the Derby Star, with which we usually train. Incidentally, it's not the first time we've used another type of ball during training sessions. This is often done in preparation for certain matches. As a coach you must always talk to your players and explain why you find that particular detail important. Players at this level usually appreciate that. Kit, boots, the ball: most players regard these things as important."

Training

On some of the other days before the confrontation with AC Milan, Ajax carries out its training sessions not on the familiar practice pitch in front of the stadium but in the stadium itself. The following is an impression of such a session, which makes clear how the Ajax team trains under Van Gaal.

The R stand has been opened to the general public, and its concrete terracing is already occupied by two soccer fans and an Italian reporter. A player walks by on the other side of the barbed wire fence. It's Ronald de Boer, who takes a series of unopposed free kicks from a distance of 20 meters, perhaps hoping that he can equal his brother's specialist skills in this area. At each attempt the ball does indeed curl into the net with admirable ease. Near post, far post; Frank is clearly his brother's twin.

Whilst the sounds of the isolated shots echo around the vacant stands, the other players trickle onto the field. Without the benefit of any warming up exercises, the players start shooting at the empty goal. A groundsman in jeans and shirt soon takes up position between the posts. Apart from the occasional ball, he doesn't really stand a chance against the projectiles flying towards him. Silooy amuses himself by teasing the despairing groundsman with cunning lobs. The exuberant mood reaches a climax when the stand-in goalkeeper loses one of his shoes and a sheepdog rushes onto the field, glad to find so many new playmates. If it weren't for the fact that players are all dressed in the same track suits, you'd swear it was just a bunch of buddies having a kick around in the local park. The dog is chased off by a group of yelling Ajax players and at last the organized warming up exercises can begin. After the practice exercises have been performed across the width of the park - timed to such perfection that synchronized swimmers would be green with envy - the official training session gets under way.

The most important practice drill is the one-two (see diagram).

A small group of players then engage in a positional game under the guidance of Gerard van der Lem. A larger group of players begins a game on one half of the pitch using a set of full-size goals. The yellows are the defending team, with Fred Grim in goal and six outfielders: Oulida, Frank de Boer, Bogarde, Reiziger,

Van den Brom and Finidi. The reds are without a goalkeeper but have an extra outfielder: Overmars, Davids, Blind, Seedorf, Wooter, Reuser and Kanu. Van Gaal is primarily interested in positional play, with the reds trying to take advantage of the extra man. From time to time, Van Gaal stops the play. His comments are frequently directed at Kanu on account of his poor movement. The game is all about advancing or staying, creating space or sprinting into a gap, playing the ball wide or forward, playing the ball back or making a run. More seems to go wrong than right, but now and then a loud compliment rings out. "Good ball, Ed," shouts Van Gaal in the direction of Davids who, without touching the ball, makes a threatening run on the inside to create space for Overmars. Overmars is left free and is indeed given the ball. Kanu is praised for running across Reuser to the near post as Overmars centers, thus distracting attention from Reuser, who finds himself free in front of goal and scores.

The roles are later reversed when Reuser draws a defender by making a diagonal run, creating space for Blind to play a ball through to the unmarked Kanu, who promptly slices the ball along the ground into the net, just as Van Basten did against Germany in 1988. Davids then tries to beat his man, but loses the ball, and the opposition nearly scores. "Don't take risks in that position", the coach instructs him, "not if there's still a man behind. Lay it back in that case".

At one point Van Gaal thinks Seedorf has made the wrong move. Their words are inaudible from the stand, but the angry exchange of gestures with the hands indicates the run of play. "Seedorf was right, on appeal," calls Van Gaal to indicate that play can be resumed. At just 19 years of age, Seedorf is in many respects a completely mature soccer player.

Van Gaal tells the reds to moderate their forward pressure. "Defend here instead of in their half," says Van Gaal, with 24 May in the back of his mind. "Let them come at you, then go on the offensive." It's noticeable that the reds do then make several attempts to pick up the yellows later. But when the reds regain possession and start their attacking buildup, under pressure from the yellows things go wrong twice in succession; they lose possession and the yellows score. The yellows win 4-2.

It is drizzling heavily when the groups join up again and start a final practice drill.

The drill is carried out on the left and on the right. Depending on whether the goalkeeper is positioned at the near or the far post, the ball has to be flighted accurately from the by-line. Both Grim and Van der Sar hold some really awkward balls. Some of the goals are rare beauties, such as one scored by Ronald de Boer, who meets a cross from the right beyond the far post and hammers the ball in with his left foot via the underside of the bar. He holds his hands aloft all the way back to the center circle. But other balls disappear behind the fencing into the empty terraces, as shots are struck high and wide. Sometimes the ball is miskicked. This happens to Kanu, provoking the obvious exasperation of the coach: "Good grief, Kanu!" But every now and again the striker puts away impossible chances, evoking equally loud praise. "The goalkeepers have won," shouts Van Gaal, and the final practice drill is concluded. Evidently he has been keeping a tally of all the saves and goals.

The approximately 150 spectators assembled in the R stand and the estimated 30 journalists in the press box notice Frank Rijkaard entering the stadium, accompanied by physio Laszlo Jambor. While Van Gaal goes off with one half of the group to practice corner kicks, and Van der Lem takes the other half to do some finishing practice, Rijkaard gracefully trots around the touch-line of the stadium to which he returned just two years ago.

Gerard van der Lem shows a group of players some finishing moves. These are executed alternately from left and right. The player who is not targeted by the cross runs in late towards the far post.

It is almost 12 o'clock, and Van Gaal's group of corner kickers leaves the field, except for Seedorf and Overmars, who do some extra drills with Van Gaal. The coach plays a ball to each of them in turn and then plays defender. They each have to go round him and shoot past Grim. The other group of players is trying out a simpler form of finishing move: the ball is simply played through the middle to Van der Lem, who lays it back diagonally for a shot. In a strip of grass in front of the main grandstand, Edgar Davids is juggling with the ball. It is as if the left midfielder is in a totally different world, his ball skills defying the laws of gravity, practicing conjuring tricks in front of the empty terraces. There is no applause, but if there were he wouldn't notice.

As soon as Overmars and Seedorf retire to the showers, Van Gaal continues to whet his insatiable appetite by firing shots at Grim, conspicuously passing the keeper on a number of occasions.

When Van der Lem's group calls it a day, the assistant coach makes his way towards Grim. With boyish enthusiasm he also lets fly at the reserve goalkeeper. The goals he scores, some of which are exquisitely finished, are, unlike Van Gaal's, accompanied by the necessary verbals: "See, that's how I always used to take them." Grim smiles but says nothing.

Rijkaard is practicing long bounding strides in another corner of the pitch. His knee must see him through at least one more match. Grim, muddy from his diving practice, saunters off the field with Van der Lem and Van Gaal.

Litmanen can be observed kicking balls towards an empty goal at the other end of the pitch. A few minutes later Bobby Haarms takes his life in his hands by going into goal. Penalties are taken, perhaps as a precaution for 24 May. The Finn would rather be prepared and, like Ronald de Boer's at the start of the training session, his shots echo loudly around the empty stadium. There's something in the air, but no one quite seems to know what it is.

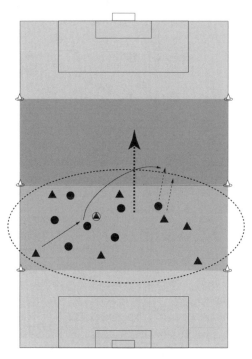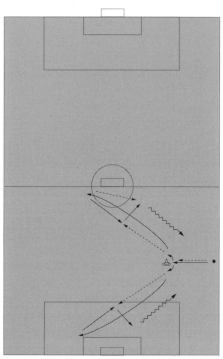

Vienna

After the final morning's training session on Monday, 22 May, the Ajax squad departs for the former political and cultural capital of Europe. The Ajax and AC Milan teams arrive at Vienna airport within minutes of each other. The difference between the teams is immediately noticeable. The AC Milan players have an aura of self-esteem and style. The youthful Ajax players stare in awe at their Italian counterparts as they stroll regally into the arrivals hall with their stunningly beautiful female companions at their side.

However, years of international youth tournaments have taught the Ajax prodigies how to cope with the charisma of their rivals. In contrast to AC Milan's swanky elegance, the Ajax players are models of repose and youthful cool. Despite the chaotic media hype, the Ajax squad remains surprisingly calm.

Before the Italians' training session in the impressive Ernst Happel stadium, AC Milan's injured Dutch star Marco van Basten is quick to praise Louis van Gaal's approach. "For me, the composure and self-confidence which Louis van Gaal exudes at such a crucial moment is one of the secrets behind the present team's success. This air of calm always transmits itself to the players, and even gets through to the opposition. The AC Milan players know that they will be facing a team with a huge amount of self-assurance. It's really something special if you can instill this attitude into such a young team. It shows that you are a top coach."

Fitness

The same can also be said of AC Milan coach Fabio Capello. He is the first coach who has succeeded in taking a team to three successive appearances in the most important European club soccer tournament. At the end of the morning's training session he manages to evade the clutches of the media. He jogs a number of laps unaccompanied around the running track of the empty but sultry Ernst Happel stadium before, perspiring, he seeks out the showers. "A sound mind in a sound body" is a maxim which also, and perhaps particularly, applies to top coaches.

The training session confirms that Capello expects the game to be won or lost in the cramped midfield. In the positional game, the key players have to harass their opponents continuously after losing possession. At all times Capello wants at least three players around the opposing player in possession. In this way Ajax's most important asset - their ability to push the ball around while retaining possession - can be neutralized.

It is significant that the Frenchman, Marcel Desailly, is not included in the first team line-up during the training session. But it's soon clear why. His job in the reserve team is to follow Zvonimir Boban wherever he goes. This is in preparation for his role in the final: to neutralize Litmanen by marking him rigidly out of the game. Or, in the words of Louis van Gaal: "Litmanen can expect to be followed everywhere by a super athlete."

The final

Early in the afternoon on 24 May, historic Vienna has already been turned into a witches' cauldron by 35,000 Italian and Dutch soccer fans, whose colorful outfits and raucous voices create a unique atmosphere.

Many soccer players and coaches are superstitious, but apprehensive Ajax fans need not worry about watching the final. The posters announce the game as AFC Ajax v AC Milan. Ajax has thus been given first billing, and since the 1969/70 season the Italians have always come off second best whenever this happened. Moreover the current AC Milan coach has a poor record against Ajax. Not only did he lose 2-0 in each of the group ties against Ajax earlier this season, but he also lost 1-0 to Ajax as a Juventus player in the 1973 final.

The pessimists, however, are quick to recall the day last season when Ajax was played off the park in an away leg at Parma. It was Ajax's worst performance under Van Gaal. Optimists, on the other hand, point out that the home game against Parma, even though it ended in a 0-0 draw, was voted by UEFA as one of the most exciting contests of the 93-94 season. In short, Ajax tends to play well against Italian opponents.

Warming-up

Well before the kick-off, Ajax and Milan start their warming up in the seething Ernst Happel stadium. Ajax operates as a team, with every player knowing exactly what he has to do. The AC Milan players only do one work-out together - running exercises in groups of two, from the edge of the penalty area to the center line, under the eyes of their running coach, plus some loosening up exercises. Otherwise each player does his own thing. The running coach assists where necessary. Defender Panucci, for example, asks the trainer to throw him the ball, and plays it back into his hands with either the right or left foot. After each throw he puts all his energy into a brief sprint on the spot. Desailly is also conspicuous on account of the enormous amount of energy he expends at the end of the warming up session by sprinting in different directions. Next to Marco van Basten on the touch-line is the disappointed Dejan Savicevic. All the Dutch dailies had reported that he would play, but on the big day the largest circulation Italian newspaper, La Gazetta dello Sport, led with the headline that the Croat would be missing from the Milan line-up. Van Gaal doesn't know whether to commiserate with his colleague Capello. At the post-match press conference he remarks: "Savicevic is unpredictable, both for the opposition and his own team. He can win a final on his own, but he can also lose it by upsetting the balance of his own team. A player like Massaro gives you more security, which can be an advantage in a final." For exactly the same reasons, Van Gaal would never consider buying a player like Romario. As far as he is concerned, every individual must subordinate his own ego to the needs of the team, even the stars.

Team kits

When a mass of balloons in the colors of UEFA, Ajax and AC Milan are released into the humid skies above Vienna at the pre-scheduled time of 8.26 p.m., something strange happens. Does the fact that all the UEFA and AC Milan balloons randomly disappear on the evening air, while the red and white balloons of Ajax cluster together like a well-disciplined team, bode well for Ajax?

When the two sides line up for the traditional team photos, it's obvious that there is also some disunity in AC Milan's kit. Marco Simone and Daniele Massaro are both wearing different boots. Massaro's boots have luminous stripes on them and Simone's are completely white. It is something that Louis van Gaal probably would not accept. Immediately prior to the final, he had even given Finidi George and Kanu a ticking off because the Nigerians wanted to play the final in new boots! Nor does Van Gaal make any exceptions when it comes to team members playing with their socks round their ankles or their shirts hanging out. "You stand out from other players by virtue of your performance. If you play as a team you need to express yourself as a single unit, and that includes the way you dress." This was one of Van Gaal's first directives when he became Ajax coach in 1991.

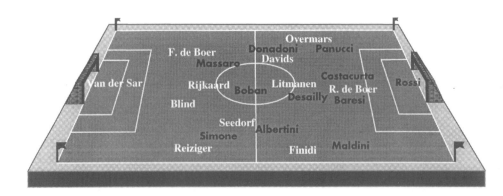

Tactics

In the first few minutes, as Van Gaal had expected, it becomes obvious that AC Milan has adopted a changed style of play to counter the threat of Ajax. When Danny Blind or Frank Rijkaard has possession, Milan striker Massaro has the task of preventing the pass to Frank de Boer or ensuring that De Boer can only move the ball wide.

This means that Ajax is forced to rely on Michael Reiziger for the initial build-up play, especially as Van der Sar has no intention of simply kicking the ball upfield in such an important match. On the night, Reiziger's form lets him down. His passes are untidy, with balls reaching the advanced striker, Ronald De Boer, at knee and chest height; De Boer is also unable to lay off enough balls to Clarence Seedorf. On the night, the right-sided midfielder who, as a 19-year-old, performed so admirably both domestically and internationally, was unable to find the right moment to move a yard or so to the left or right to play the one-two with De Boer, or to create space to accept a pass from Reiziger or Rijkaard. In the absence of these important build-up triangles on the right, Blind tries to compensate by frequently playing the ball directly to Finidi George, and with the lack of options on the left in the first half, Ajax is rarely able to practice its favorite tactic of circulating the ball. Other consequences of the tactical choices made by both teams become clear. The powerhouse of the AC Milan team, Desailly, carries out his task of marking Jari Litmanen out of the game to perfection. It eventually earns him the UEFA prize of 'Man of the Match', although only one player really came into contention for this, Frank Rijkaard, who was outstanding in his last big international appearance.

It is also significant that Boban pressures Frank Rijkaard from the very first minute when the Ajax player is in possession. AC Milan is indeed playing the diamond formation that Van Gaal had hoped for in midfield, but it is obvious that

Ajax is having problems dealing with it.

Louis van Gaal analyzes the problems of the first half as follows: "We expected AC Milan to change their game, which meant that we should have been superior to AC Milan in the first half. It quickly became clear, however, that Ajax was exhibiting less self-confidence and aggression than AC Milan. In these situations, the fact that you're tactically the better side doesn't make any difference. Besides, we made a big tactical error in midfield, which I noticed three minutes into the game. I'd read in all the papers that Boban's only task would be to prevent Rijkaard gaining possession. That was the case to start with, just as Simone tried to prevent Blind from becoming involved in the build-up play. But in fact the main purpose of the Italians' tactics was to use their diamond formation in midfield to force the build-up play to take place via Reiziger. At that moment AC Milan chose to play a pressing game, but from other positions than usual. Even so, we had the most problems. This wasn't just Reiziger's fault. He couldn't get the ball to Rijkaard, because Seedorf closed off the space. At the moment a pass was made, Ronald de Boer often found himself on the wrong side of the ball and Litmanen was cornered by Desailly. Before the interval, I went three times to the touch-line and gave instructions to Seedorf on how we should confront the problem. Seedorf was told to play 5 yards further forward and Rijkaard 5 yards further back. In that way Rijkaard would have more space, because Boban would never play so far forward. Reiziger then had two channels of play rather than one before half-time. If Simone then went to mark Rijkaard, Blind would become our extra man. It was all to do with the extra man, since Baresi was certainly not going to play in front of his defense.

At half-time I tried to instill some more self-confidence into the side and I elaborated on the solution to the problem I've just outlined. In the second half we adjusted much better and we were able to control the play."

Changeover

In their preparations for the game, Ajax may well have based all its training on being able to switch quickly into attack in a small strip around the center line once the ball had been won. This evening, however, that situation hardly materializes, providing yet more proof that, as a coach, despite all the pre-planned tactical refinements, you are totally dependent on the form of your players on the night. If seven of your players are performing below par, as was the case with Ajax in the first half of the final, the coach is stuck in the dug-out, powerless to do anything about it. You don't know where to start correcting the situation, as everything seems to be going wrong. The melee of people around you, plus the noise generated by the sets of supporters, hardly gives you a chance to turn things round.

AC Milan is therefore able to dominate play in the first half. The Italians are able to present a lesson in soccer perfection when it comes to rapidly switching the play when they gain possession. AC Milan is able to penetrate the Ajax defense with fast moves, superior strength and perfect manipulation of the ball. Their passing with the outside of the foot is outstanding. AC Milan's elegant play also demonstrates that, in the modern game, a team can be at its most vulnerable when it is in possession. Unless strict discipline is maintained, loss of possession will be instantaneously punished.

In the first half, Ajax's attempts at a counterattack look static, compared with those of AC Milan. A week after the final tie, Louis van Gaal has a different view of things. "It wasn't difficult for the Italians to switch rapidly to attack. We were losing the ball to AC Milan's midfielders and strikers. If you lose the ball in these positions, your opponents can get the ball in front of goal very quickly. If your wingers lose the ball in the corners of the pitch, then even the Italians can't switch over to attack so quickly. It is the place where possession is lost that is so vital!"

Capello's team manages to translate its dominance in the first half into two chances, but Ajax's traditional luck stays with goalkeeper Van der Sar and the Dutchmen are able to reach half-time without going a goal down.

Half-time

The fifteen minutes during the interval provide the coach with his last chance to turn a miserable run of play into a positive game. Van Gaal draws inspiration from a life-size portrait of Ernst Happel in the dressing room. The Austrian grand master of the soccer coaching world could always manage to turn a match around completely by instigating a few essential innovations. Van Gaal must hope that his legendary colleague will provide him with inspiration in the few moments available to him.

After the match, Van Gaal reveals that, at that moment, he addressed his players with mixed feelings. On the one hand he knows that superior opponents, who cannot turn their dominance into goals, often get into difficulties. On the other

hand, he is furious that so many players have flunked at the crucial moment. In the first 45 minutes, the AC Milan goalkeeper Rossi hasn't been troubled by a single Ajax shot on goal. He is the first opposing goalkeeper who has been able to say that this season.

Van Gaal also senses that his players regard the first half as a collective failure. Most of the players are acutely disappointed. He knows that he has to work at rebuilding their self-confidence.

At that decisive moment it becomes clear why Van Gaal has expended so much energy on team building. The coach isn't the only one who champions the cause. The whole group accepts responsibility. Back in the dressing room it is Frank Rijkaard who, against his instinct, has the first word. Quite composed, and without anger, he says "I want the ball to be played around faster, and a number of players need to play better when we have possession. There's no point in criticizing Reiziger. He has too few options when he gets the ball." This signals the start of a short, more heated discussion, in which Blind, Seedorf and De Boer are chiefly involved. The coach is happy to let them continue.

Van Gaal eventually takes over, adding his support to the criticism, but also giving a number of new instructions. The most important: Frank Rijkaard must see more of the ball so that he can create more threatening situations. In order to do this he will have to drop back a few yards, with the aim of forcing Boban to decide between pressuring Rijkaard or going over to positional (zonal) man-to-man marking. As it turns out, this choice proves to be highly effective after the disappointing first half. After the match, all the Ajax players felt that Rijkaard was much more in the picture in the second half. The statistics don't support this view: in the first half Rijkaard had 40 ball contacts, and in the second 41. What is different, however, is that from his 'new' position Rijkaard is able to make 8 menacing passes, 4 more than in the first half.

The figures on Rijkaard's game reveal yet another startling statistic: in the entire match he only commits one foul, and in fact there are only 30 fouls in the whole match, despite its importance to both teams. It goes to show that, in today's game, you can defend at the highest levels of the game without losing possession of the ball, i.e. giving away free kicks.

Second half

After the interval, the course of the game changes dramatically. All of a sudden, Ajax is able to practice its circulation soccer. The statistics support this view with Ajax having 60% possession and AC Milan only 40%.

Extremely satisfying for Van Gaal is the fact that, throughout the season, at 59% per game, Ajax has had by far the most possession of all the clubs in the Champions League, beating Johan Cruyff's Barcelona by 4%.

Van Gaal soon has the confidence to make tactical changes in the second half. After just 8 minutes, a visibly disappointed Seedorf is substituted. With De Boer now operating in the right midfield position, there are more options for passing the ball. Reiziger's performance promptly improves. After a number of encouraging runs from Kanu, Baresi does his utmost at the back of the defense to avoid direct confrontation with the Nigerian. The whole AC Milan team is forced to drop back 15 yards.

Whether Van Gaal is inspired by voodoo practitioners or Kluivert's mother, he makes the decision in the 70th minute to replace Litmanen, who still hasn't managed to shake off Desailly, with Patrick Kluivert. Names no longer count. For Van Gaal the team is paramount.

Substitution

"Litmanen is usually the type of player who can shake off his direct opponent. His greatest strength is his excellent timing and movement, but the physically stronger Desailly can match him any time.

Kluivert is more imaginative and creative than Litmanen. This forced Desailly to work a lot harder once Kluivert came on, and that was to our advantage. Kluivert is also a stronger header of the ball, which gives you more chances at goal through the air. That's a great bonus when, at that stage of the game, you're the stronger team."

The change around means that Ajax now have five ball-winners and five predominantly attacking players, a ratio that goes against all international soccer norms, according to which even a 7:3 ratio in favor of ball-winners is often regarded as daring. It is a gamble that can only be taken when all eleven players know what their job is when the opposition has possession. After the game, Fabio Capello admitted that his players didn't have enough time to respond to Van Gaal's tactical brinkmanship. In all fairness, you could put it another way: willingness to take risks in such a confrontation, Van Gaal won the day in Vienna against an opponent who put his faith in safety first, Capello. One of AC Milan's

most creative players, Lentini, spent most of the game on the bench, and only came on when the game had been decided, i.e. after Rijkaard's golden pass sent Kluivert through to score the goal which, together with his tears of joy, won the hearts of many a soccer fan.

"Who dares wins" is the lesson which Capello learnt to his cost after his 3rd European Cup Final in as many years.

Perfectionist

After an hour and a half of leaping, shouting and dancing off the emotions of a whole season, Van Gaal sits down to the customary press conference to reaffirm his belief in the Ajax philosophy. While explaining to the international press why it had in principle been to Ajax's advantage that AC Milan used an irregular diamond pattern in midfield, he takes the time to make sure that the UEFA interpreter translates his words accurately. This is typical of the perfectionist Van Gaal.

Some moments later an Italian journalist asks if he now considers himself to be the all-time top Dutch coach.

Van Gaal replies, "Ask me that question in seven years, when I'm 50. At the moment my record can't compare with the achievements of Rinus Michels, who made an enormous contribution to Dutch soccer during his career. Before the Michels era Dutch soccer had very little to offer. The international breakthrough was due to Michels." This statement typifies Van Gaal's deep respect for his colleague Rinus Michels, but also indicates his own ambitions. The impressive honors list of two Dutch championships, one national cup competition, one UEFA Cup and victory in the Champions' League in the short period of three years is just a beginning.

Ajax players celebrate their champions League Final Victory over AC Milan.

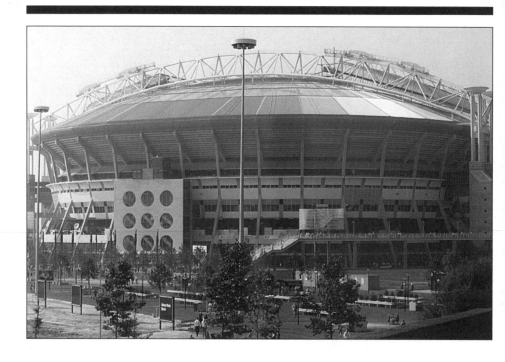

Chapter 11
The Last Tour de Force

On 22 November, 1995, Danny Blind scores the goal that makes Ajax the World Club Champions at the cost of Brazil's Grémio. At the celebrations on Amsterdam's Museumplein, Louis van Gaal can therefore proclaim Ajax's superiority, as the best club in the world, over arch rivals Feyenoord, Rotterdam and PSV Eindhoven.

A fitting end to the most successful year in Ajax's history. Dutch Champion, winner of the Dutch Cup and the European Super Cup, winner of the Champions League, winner of the World Club Championship. It is hard to imagine a more impressive list of achievements. The whole of the Netherlands supports Ajax. Van Gaal even receives letters of congratulation from Feyenoord fans, who usually only use the name Ajax as a term of abuse. Young girls swoon in adoration of the young Adonises of the Ajax team, just as they once did for their favorite pop stars. The Ajax hype takes on previously unimagined dimensions, both inside and outside the Netherlands.

But, as so often in history, the high point also revealed the first signs of the coming decline.

"The game in Tokyo against Grémio was played largely to satisfy commercial interests, and with hindsight I feel we could have done without it. The trip, coming at the end of such a strenuous year, took a lot out of the players. Tokyo laid the basis for the wave of injuries in 1996, with all its consequences."

After the winter break in the Dutch soccer season, it soon became apparent that the Japanese trip had been too much of a good thing and would be paid for dearly. In the run-up to the second half of the season the Ajax players again learned what it is like to lose. In the training camp in Israel, the team lost unexpectedly to Maccabi Haifa. This defeat was promptly followed by another in the Dutch league game against Willem II Tilburg. Cambuur, a team from a lower division, knocked Ajax out of the Dutch Cup competition, and more league games were lost, to Vitesse Arnhem and Roda JC Kerkrade. Suddenly all of Ajax's opponents felt that they had a chance.

Setbacks never occur singly. The brother of right winger Finidi George was shot dead in Nigeria. Patrick Kluivert was involved in a fatal car accident, and when it was found that he had been driving too fast he was suddenly the focus of intense adverse media attention. Van Gaal dealt with these events in his own typical manner. He ensured that the players were given all the support they needed within the club, and shielded his charges as best he could from the outside world.

Then Davids and Reiziger announced that they were leaving to join AC Milan. The newly won freedom of movement of players at the end of their

contract period thus took its first toll of Ajax. Van Gaal made no attempt to hide his emotions when he took leave of his two young stars, as was the case when Rijkaard and Pettersson also departed. This typified his relationship with his players.

Marc Overmars, so crucial for Ajax's attacking play, sustained a bad knee injury, which put him out of action for months. His successor Martijn Reuser broke his leg one week later. Ajax bought Peter Hoekstra as a replacement, but he was ineligible to play in the European Cup.

Van Gaal's achievement in winning the Dutch league championship after all these setbacks was of the very highest order. The media had expected PSV Eindhoven to win, but in the end Van Gaal triumphed yet again, to the joy of the club's legion of fans. Ajax even succeeded in reaching the final of the Champions League, for the second season in succession. This time, however, its Italian opponent, Juventus Turin, was able to dictate the game. Ajax was out-classed at times and it was a small wonder that the team held until the penalty shoot-out. Two of the players who were to leave the club, Davids and Silooy, missed from the penalty spot. Ferrara, Pessotto, Padovano and Jugovic kept their nerve and won the most important European soccer cup for Juventus.

It seemed that the time had come for Van Gaal to take his leave of Ajax. He had had so may successes and built up so much credit that any successor would have faced an almost impossible task at that moment. The international soccer

world lay at the feet of the most successful coach in Ajax's long history. Why should he stay for another year with a squad that had lost so many quality players?

Nevertheless, Van Gaal stayed. There were two reasons. On 17 January, 1994, he had suffered his own personal tragedy when his wife died after a long drawn out illness. During the afternoon he sat in the dug-out at the game between Ajax and MVV Maastricht, fulfilling his duties as a coach, and in the evening he and his daughters, Brenda and Renata, took leave of Fernanda. Everyone at Ajax closed ranks around Van Gaal and his children, supporting them to the utmost in their time of need. The man who had so often shielded his players was now himself shielded and helped. At that time Van Gaal decided that he would not take up a coaching position abroad until his daughters were ready for this step. At the end of 1995 this was not the case, and he therefore went into the 1996-97 season as coach of Ajax, although it was almost predictable that he had nothing to win and almost everything to lose.

One challenge that he certainly looked forward to was playing in the new Ajax stadium, which, after much discussion, was given the name ArenA. The atmosphere at the old De Meer stadium on the Amsterdamse Middenweg had been unique, and the stadium was virtually holy ground, but it no longer measured up to the requirements of a top club. The ArenA was presented as the latest wonder of the world in the field of stadium architecture. The scale of the opening celebrations matched those for the Olympic Games. Season tickets for one year changed hands for tens of thousands of dollars. Plans for alternative uses for seats that were not sold were definitively scrapped. Ajax was assured of crowds of 50,000 for each home game for years to come. There are waiting lists for the high-priced business seats. Ajax was again a trendsetter, and the optimism in Amsterdam knew no bounds.

But 1996 proved an unlucky year for the club's new home, too. From the very beginning there were problems with the grass surface, which is so important for Ajax's cultivated style of play. This was a subject of constant criticism in the media. Nature cannot always be persuaded to advance with the speed of a computer. Loyal Ajax fans were unhappy about the seat prices and the expensive Ajax card that has to be acquired if you want to eat or drink in the ArenA.

The Ajax first team squad was also scathing about the new ArenA during the first months. In De Meer everything had been familiar, and everything was done to further the interests of Ajax and only Ajax. Anyone who disagreed with this state of affairs could pack his bags. The ArenA, however, is multi-functional, and the management has to please more customers than just Ajax. A lavish corporate presentation, or a concert by a megastar is then more important than a training session by Ajax. On such occasions there is a clash of interests, certainly when the perfectionist Van Gaal is involved, who tries to leave nothing to chance - not even an "ordinary" day's training. Training sessions sometimes have to be interrupted so that the players can move their cars. In the days of the old stadium, Van Gaal would have woken up at night in a cold sweat if he had dreamt that such a thing could happen. In ArenA it is suddenly reality. The first weeks of the new season were therefore particularly trying for everyone at Ajax. The results on the field were also giving cause for alarm. In mid August, 1996, Van Gaal, who has never been scared to prophesy success or failure, both to his players and to the media, announces that Ajax can expect to have a poor season. He can justify his pessimism simply by pointing to his squad of players, which has been drastically thinned out after a dramatic pre-season preparation period. During the traditional training camp, Litmanen, Reuser, Overmars, Kluivert, Hoekstra, Veldman and Bogarde had to sit on the sidelines because of injuries. This was the start of the worst Ajax period since the 1950s. At no time during the rest of the year could Van Gaal pick more than eight of the players that he had thought of as forming his basic team before the start of this catastrophic season. This team would have read as follows: Van der Sar; Veldman, Blind, Frank de Boer, Bogarde; Ronald de Boer, Litmanen, Witschge; Babangida, Kluivert, Overmars. On many occasions Van Gaal was glad to have six or seven members of this team available. In particular, the injuries to the players who formed the backbone of the team - Blind, Litmanen and Kluivert - proved crucial, and Ajax suddenly lost one game after the other, both in the Dutch league and at European level. At some training sessions Van Gaal had only three of his first team players available. The others were either injured or had been called up to play for their countries.

For the first time in many years, Ajax was out of the running for the Dutch league championship by mid-season. Tiny Heracles knocked the club out of the

Dutch Cup, and the Dutch Super Cup was won by PSV Eindhoven, who defeated Ajax in the ArenA by the embarrassing margin of 3-0.

Soon there was only one objective open to the club - to maintain its European challenge after the winter break. The day of decision was 4 December, in Zurich. Only a win could help against the Grasshoppers. During the preceding days Van Gaal gave everything that he could as a top coach. He talked at length with each player individually. There were more group discussions than usual. Now that the need was greatest, he made optimal use of one of the tools whose importance he had emphasized when he first came to Ajax - mutual communication.

Even in this crucial game, Van Gaal remained true to his principles. Under extremely difficult circumstances he remained stoical, emanated confidence in the team's ability to achieve a good result. Again he refused to be swayed by names or reputations. The expensive newcomers - Santos, Juan, Dani and Gabrich - were left out. Products of the Ajax youth development system, such as Splinter, Melchiot, Reuser and Musampa played instead. In particular, the choice of the inexperienced Splinter instead of the "World Champion" Santos was questioned by the international press. After the game Van Gaal explained. "Santos is a better defender than Splinter, but defending was not an option in this game. We had to win. In such a situation the first pass out of defense is of crucial importance. You must not lose the ball. Splinter is better at keeping the ball than Santos, and, even though he is still young, he is better at sizing up when he can make a forward run out of the defensive line to take up a position to receive the ball."

Van Gaal was again proved right. Thanks to an enormous physical effort, the Ajax players won 74 of the 116 tackles, and some luck in the nail bitingly exciting second half, Ajax came through and thus had something to play for in the last four months of the Van Gaal era. Ajax miraculously reached the semi-final of the Champions League before falling to a stronger and healthier Juventus side.

On 10 October, 1996, Louis van Gaal announced that he would be leaving Ajax at the end of the 1996-97 season. Even CNN reported the announcement in its World News. This was just one of many confirmations of Van Gaal's unique achievement in just five years at "his" Ajax. In Van Gaal's words, "I was born here, played for Ajax myself, worked as youth coach and assistant coach, and was given the chance, as chief coach, to change the whole structure of the club. I was able to adjust the squad of players in accordance with my own insights. I view Ajax as my life's work. At the next club I will simply be passing through. I have no idea where I will go. Perhaps I will take a year's leave. I will not know until the end of the season. But one thing will always be clear to me, and that is that I owe everything to one club: Ajax."

The long awaited announcement came on June 30th, 1997, Louis van Gaal, and assistants Gerard van der Lem and Frans Hoek, had signed a three year contract to coach the legendary Spanish club Barcelona.

On 10 October, 1996, Louis van Gaal announced that he would be leaving Ajax at the end of the 1996-97 season. Even CNN reported the announcement in its World News. This was just one of the many confirmations of Van Gaal's unique achievement in just just five years at "his" Ajax. In Van Gaal's words, "I was born here, played for Ajax myself, worked as youth coach and assistant coach, and was given the chance, as chief coach, to change the whole structure of the club I will simply be passing though. I have no idea where I will go. Perhaps I will take a year's leave. i will not know until the end of the season. But one thing will always be clear to me, and that is that I owe everything to one club: Ajax."

Suggested Coaching Reference Material

Videos
The Dutch Soccer School: Part 1: 40 offensive Drills for Attacking Soccer
The Dutch Soccer School: Part 2: Attacking From the Back
The Dutch Soccer School: Part 3 Defending
Coaching The Italian 4:4:2 with Arrigo Sacchi
Brazilian Soccer Skills and Tactics with Zico
German Skills and Small Sided Games with Otto Baric
Training Soccer Champions with Anson Dorrance
The Soccer Goalkeeper with Frans Hoek
Small Sided Games for Functional Training (Italian)
The Dutch Soccer School: Part 4: Conditioning for Soccer
Soccer Fundamentals with Wiel Coerver

Books
Dutch Soccer Drills: Part 1 Individual Skills
Dutch Soccer Drills: Part 2 Combinational Play and Small Sided Games
Team Building by Henny Kormelink and Tjeu Seeverens
Developing Soccer Players: The Dutch Way by Henny Kormelink and Tjeu Seeverens
The Manual of Soccer Coaching by Roy Rees
Coaching Soccer: Ages 5-12 by Andy Caruso
Soccer's Dynamic Short Sided Games by Andy Caruso
The Complete Handbook of Conditioning for Soccer
The Dutch Soccer Notebook

These books and videos and many others are available from REEDSWAIN SOCCER BOOKS and VIDEOS. To order or to get a free catalog call 1-800-331-5191

More great soccer books
from REEDSWAIN

Developing Soccer Players: The Dutch Way

Developing Soccer
Players: The Dutch Way
$12.95

The Dutch Coaching Notebook

The Dutch Coaching
Notebook
The Ultimate Companion for
Coaches at All Levels
$14.95

Playing Out of Your Mind

Playing Out of Your Mind
*A Soccer Player and
Coach's Guide to
Developing Mental
Toughness*
by Dr. Alan Goldberg
$9.95

Coaching The Italian 4:4:2 and Zone Play

Coaching The Italian
4:4:2 and Zone Play
$14.95
*by Floriano Marziali
and Vincenzo Mora*

Team Building

Team Building
$9.95

612 Pughtown Road
Spring City, Pennsylvania
19475
1-800-331-5191